The
Conflict of Homonyms
in English

BY

EDNA REES WILLIAMS

ARCHON BOOKS
1970

[*Yale Studies in English, Vol. 100*]

SBN: 208 00919 1
Library of Congress Catalog Card Number: 70-91193
Printed in the United States of America

TO

MY MOTHER

AND THE MEMORY OF

MY FATHER

PREFACE

IN a warring and troubled world, a study of words seems strangely remote from men's chief concerns. But the author of the following study likes to remember that some of the great men of the world have, in times that were disturbed and filled with conflict, found it worth while to compile glossaries and write books for the study of grammar, and to investigate the functions and meanings of words. King Alfred established a long tradition when, in the midst of the manifold affairs of his troubled kingdom, he made time to study for himself his native English language and to plan for the teaching of it. The Danes were thronging into England while Ælfric wrote his *Grammar*. There were more than rumors of wars in the years when scholars were preparing many volumes of the *New English Dictionary*. Wars and conquests disturb all such pursuits; but among the results of wars and conquests are changes in language and the traveling of words. The English language is even now, as the result of wars and the movements of armies, undergoing change and taking to itself many new words. As new words come in, old ones frequently vanish. There is an ever-renewed interest, and perhaps a real value even in the midst of war, in the study of the histories of words and the people who use them.

The work that follows is an investigation of one cause of the loss of words, the possible effect on the English vocabulary of the conflict of homonyms. It is an application of the principles of linguistic geography to a study of certain phenomena in the English language, an extension of the methods established by the French scholar Jules Gilliéron and his followers in their investigations of French dialects. As the principles involved and the plan of the book are discussed in detail in the Introduction, they need not be explained further here. The book was, in its original form, a dissertation begun and carried on at the suggestion and under the direction of Professor Robert J. Menner, and presented in partial fulfillment of the requirements for the degree of Doctor of Philosophy in Yale University.

To Professor Menner I wish to express my deepest gratitude for uncounted benefits not to be forgot. His willingness to help in the many difficulties that surrounded my investigations, especially in their early stages, was unfailing; his searching and forthright criticism of all parts of the book was indispensable; his patience in the delays to which the work was subjected was, apparently, unlimited. And my indebtedness to him extends beyond the bounds of one book, of one piece of work. From the day when as a student in his class I began the study of Old English, to the present time, his counsel and assistance, repeatedly sought, have been freely given. His learning, his keen awareness of the true values of scholarship, are in themselves a source of inspiration and guidance to those who have the good fortune to work with him.

I wish to express my thanks also to Professor Max Förster, of Munich, whose careful reading of my manuscript and written notes and comments on various items in it have been of help to me; to Professor Rudolph Willard for assistance and kindness shown in many ways; to my brother, Arthur Rees Williams, for the reproduction of the maps which accompany these studies; and to the members of the staff of the Yale University Library for many kindnesses. Of a different nature is my debt of gratitude to three others whose names I wish to add here—the late Professor Josiah Bethea Game and Professor William G. Dodd, to whose teaching and friendship I owe much, and the late Professor Raymond Wilson Chambers, of London, through whose conversation and lectures my interest in the whole field of Germanic language and literature and thought was quickened and deepened.

The Committee on Publication of the Department of English of Yale University has approved my manuscript for publication in the Yale Studies in English; to the members of that committee and to Yale University I express my appreciation of the subvention which makes possible the appearance of this book at the present time. To Professor Benjamin C. Nangle I express my thanks for his careful and generous assistance in preparing the manuscript for the press.

E. R. W.

Northampton, Massachusetts,
  June 18, 1943.

CONTENTS

LIST OF MAPS

INTRODUCTION

I

The Theory of Homonymic Conflict

i. Definition and Example

THE reasons for the disappearance of words from a particular language are to be sought in various phases of the history of that language and of the people who speak it. Explanations are necessarily numerous and diverse. The theory of the conflict of homonyms is one of such explanations. It is the theory, now demonstrated to that point of scientific accuracy and thoroughness at which the word *theory* may be replaced by *principle,* that attributes the loss, or change in form or status, of certain individual words to the confusion that arises from their being identical in sound, or becoming identical through normal phonological development, with other words established within the same sphere of thought and usage and so admitting of confusion. It embraces a study of the phonological processes by which words attain homonymy and the investigation of all the ways by which a given language changes, or provides against, situations in which such confusion between words is possible.

Phonetic identity is basic to the principle. Similarity in sound is not sufficient ground on which to admit words to studies of homonymic conflict, for it is an accepted principle that the phonemes of a language, though they may and do vary from period to period, within one period are distinct entities and are recognized as distinct by the speakers of that period.[1] Thus the close and open *ẹ̄* [eː] and *ę̄* [ɛː] of Middle English times may seem, to people of a later age, to have been closely similar; but the two sounds were, through centuries of their history, clearly differentiated. Middle English (West Saxon) *brẹ̄de* 'to roast' and *brę̄de* 'to breed' were not homophones. Only when words are, in themselves, exactly alike phonetically or when they become so in certain common speech-constructions are they subject to mutual conflict.

There have been, it is true, instances of interference between words that are not true homophones; similarity in sound may, under particular circumstances, be the cause of confusion and so lead to homonymic attraction or to conflict. But instances of the kind are, on the whole, exceptional, and proof of the occurrence of conflict must, in such cases, be singularly clear.[2]

1. Leonard Bloomfield, *Language* (New York, 1933), pp. 74 ff.
2. See Jules Gilliéron and Mario Roques, *Études de géographie linguistique* (Paris, 1912), p. 11: ". . . la forte ressemblance peut jouer dans l'histoire d'un mot un rôle

Equally fundamental to the theory is the possibility of confusion between words. This does not mean that homophones inevitably conflict. "A language does not tolerate homophones," or, as Sir Robert Bridges expresses the same idea, "Homophones are a nuisance,"[3] is not a true statement, as even the most hurried observation of the English vocabulary will make clear. Homophones do exist, and have existed for centuries, side by side in the language without causing confusion, ambiguity, or even inconvenience. There is little probability that one hearing such a sentence as "He will write a letter" will understand for *write* any one of its three homophones *right, rite, wright,* or will even think of them. The verb *well* and its related substantive *well* have not interfered with the adverb and adjective *well,* nor are they likely to do so. The verb *heal* and the substantive *heel* are not mutually antagonistic. But when words within the same general sphere of thought, words common to one or other particular social stratum, words that are similarly construed in sentences or phrases are homonyms, or develop homonymy through normal phonetic changes, then confusion and conflict are likely to ensue between them, to the detriment or loss of one or more of them. "L'homonymie n'est pas une force qui va, fatale, inéluctable, détruisant sans merci tout ce que lui livre une phonétique aveugle: pour qu'elle ait à agir, encore faut-il qu'il y ait rencontre, et la rencontre ne se produit que pour des mots engagés dans les mêmes chemins de la pensée."[4]

The student of the conflict of homonyms must keep constantly in mind this question of the habitat, so to speak, of the several words—the background of social conditions and geographical, historical, and psychological factors influencing the lives of the people and, in turn, the language that they speak. A word used by the farming classes of the North of England will, quite evidently, not come into conflict with a literary word of the educated classes of London, though both in their sphere may be common words. A word pertaining to ships and the life of seamen will not be confused with one that is essentially an agricultural term.[5] A term that became obsolete in England in the fourteenth century cannot have been influenced by a Renaissance loan-word of Elizabethan England. Lines of demarcation in usage

égal ou presque égal à celui de l'homonymie parfaite." E. Öhmann states clearly his opinion that paronymy, as well as full homonymy, may exert a disturbing influence on the development of words, citing as evidence the phenomena of folk-etymology and attraction: *Über Homonymie und Homonyme im Deutschen,* in *Annales Academiæ Scientiarum Fennicæ,* Series B, 32, 1 (Helsinki, 1934), 1–143.

3. Sir Robert Bridges, *On English Homophones,* Society for Pure English, Tract II (Oxford, 1919), p. 18.

4. Gilliéron and Roques, *Études de géographie linguistique,* pp. 149–50.

5. Compare, for example, the verbs *rake* (*NED,* v.³) used of masts or funnels of ships and meaning 'to incline from the perpendicular,' and *rake* (*NED,* v.¹) 'to collect with, or as with, a rake.'

such as these are fairly distinct and not difficult to discover. But there are less evident, finer lines of distinction that are not always easily to be determined. Even within the same general social and intellectual sphere, homonymous words are very frequently distinguished by the grammatical and syntactical constructions in which they are commonly used. Only under unusual circumstances will a substantive meet interference from a verb, or even an intransitive from a transitive verb. Numerous examples are at hand in the living English vocabulary to support this statement: the substantive *fly* and the verb *fly;* the adjective *red* and the past tense and participle of *read,* verb; the adjective *limp* and the verb *limp; rest,* commonly an intransitive verb, and *wrest,* transitive (except obsolete intransitive uses).[6] Connotation and sentence-connections—those ideas and expressions with which certain words are commonly associated—even intonation, may serve effectively to distinguish some words from their homonyms. Only when the words concerned are alike in sound, when they are in common use in the same social and intellectual circles, and when they perform the same syntactical functions in the language, within a common sphere of ideas, do they become, in general, subject to mutual confusion and to conflict.[7]

One or two examples cited from studies of homonyms in French will show more succinctly than mere explanation can the principle of homonymic conflict. One of the most clear-cut and easily explained instances, the classic example, is that of the words meaning 'cock' and 'cat' in southwestern France.[8] Latin *cattus* 'cat' became in all this section of France *gat.* In the greater part of the same section the terms used to designate the cock are derivatives of Latin *gallus* (*gal, galo, dzau, djyal,* etc.), except for two small areas where *gallus* does not persist, the words for 'cock' in one being derivatives of *pullus,* and in the other *vicaire* or *faisan.* A form of *gallus* does appear at

6. Two points of consideration come close together here and must be kept distinct. Some words are distinguished from their homophones from the very beginning of their history by particular syntactical constructions or other limitations. On the other hand, words are not infrequently restricted to particular phrases or constructions or to certain semantic spheres as the result of the effort of a people to avoid the ambiguity arising from homonymy. This is one of the methods, shortly to be discussed in greater detail, by which confusion is avoided. The chronology of all the factors involved is here, as it is throughout any study of the conflict of homonyms, of the utmost importance.

7. There are instances in which the influence of words may cross, has indeed crossed, these limits and caused interference with other words not so definitely of the same level; these are usually words of unpleasant meaning, pejorative significance, obscene connotation. Such words may bring about the loss of others in good standing merely by being like them in sound. See Karl Jaberg, *Sprachgeographie* (Aarau, 1908), pp. 11–13 and Map 10; and E. Öhmann, "Die Präposition AFTER im Deutschen," *PBB,* LV (1931), 230–43.

8. Gilliéron and Roques, *Études de géographie linguistique,* pp. 121 ff. and Map XII. Only part of the discussion is reproduced here.

one point far to the south and west of the *faisan* area; this, together with the fact that representatives of the feminine *gallina* are still to be found throughout the area, makes it appear probable that *gallus* also, at one time, was used everywhere. It disappeared from the areas where *vicaire, faisan,* and *pullus* (part of this area) appear, because of the conflict of homonyms. In just those sections, final *-ll* from Vulgar Latin *-ll-* normally became *-t;* thus *gallus* would there have become *gat,* and those dialects would in consequence have had two words *gat:*

But **gat* 'cock' would have, or did, come into immediate conflict with *gat* 'cat,' both being the names of familiar domestic animals and so particularly subject to mutual confusion in the ordinary language of domestic circles. Both, however, did not survive. The word for 'cat' was the more firmly established term, and so held its place. For **gat* 'cock' substitutes were found.

A more complicated but equally convincing instance is that of the collision of the words *épi* (*de blé*) and *épine* in southwestern France.[9] Its main points may be mentioned here; only a study, such as that made by Gilliéron and Roques, of each detail of the maps constructed on data from the *Atlas linguistique de la France*[10] can show all the history of the "rencontre." *Épi,* the ordinary French term for 'spike (of wheat),' is a derivative of Latin *spicum.* Various derivative forms of this word and of Latin *spica* are used in this meaning throughout France, except in a small section in the extreme southwest. In this section the ordinary dialectal form is *kabel,* a word in no way related to the other two.[11] *Épine* is the French word for 'thorn,' derived from Latin *spina.* It is used throughout France, except in a section in the southwest, where it is replaced by other words— *brok, beuk, tyak,* etc. The areas in which these two common and similar but historically unrelated words are displaced by completely dissimilar forms are almost coincident. The explanation of this striking fact lies in the phonological history of *spicum* 'spike (of wheat)' and *spina* 'thorn.' The two terms came into conflict in that particular area through normal phonological developments. *Spicum* there took the form *espi;* and *spina* also became *espi,* through loss of the intervocalic nasal, a process quite definitely restricted to this southwest corner of France. Thus *espi* meant both 'spike of wheat' and

9. Gilliéron and Roques, *Études de géographie linguistique,* pp. 132 ff. and Maps XIII, 2 and 4.

10. Jules Gilliéron and E. Edmont, *L'Atlas linguistique de la France,* Paris, 1902–10.
11. See the following section.

'thorn.' But these are terms of not infrequent occurrence in the language of rural communities, that is, they come within the same realm of ideas and are likely to occur in proximity in ordinary conversation; in the words of the authors, "mots ruraux, mots de la technique du cultivateur, désignant tous deux des formations végétales, des excroissances plus ou moins piquantes, ils appartenaient à des classes sémantiques voisines, à des groupes intimement liés, peut-être par occasion au même groupe. . . ."[12] Conflict between them under the circumstances was certain. And examination of the present dialectal distribution of all the words leads to the inevitable conclusion that such conflict resulted in the loss of both terms from that very area in which they normally became homonyms. *Espi* 'spike of wheat' was replaced by *kabel*, a metaphorical expression; *espi* 'thorn,' by words not at all like it in sound.

Instances might be cited at length from the work of Gilliéron, his students, and other scholars interested in his methods. These two illustrate the general principle. But they do not show all the implications, the corollaries, of the theory of homonymic conflict. Especially interesting are the various effects of such conflict on the vocabulary; to discuss these one must mention certain principles and conceptions of linguistic geography, such as that of the traveling of words, Gilliéron's "voyages des mots," which are more or less closely related to them.

ii. Effects of Conflict on Vocabulary
Corollaries of the Theory

Conflict between two words may result in the complete loss of one of them, as in the case of *°gat* 'cock,' or of both, as in that of *espi* 'spike of wheat' and *espi* 'thorn.' It may, again, result in the limiting of one of the words to specific meanings, to particular syntactical constructions—so-called "petrified phrases"—or to certain particular combinations of words in which the term, elsewhere ambiguous, is clearly understood. And again conflict may lead to formal changes in the word or words concerned, or establish in common use variant forms already in existence, the process that Gilliéron and others after him have called "la pathologie et thérapeutique des mots."[1]

Loss of Words and Substitute Terms. The Traveling of Words. The loss of words is, theoretically, the simplest of the results, but it is not simple in its final effect on the vocabulary. The word or words

---

12. Gilliéron and Roques, *Études de géographie linguistique*, p. 150.
1. Other effects have, by various writers on the subject, been observed. Öhmann, for example, traces certain variations in the gender of German nouns to conflict, or potential conflict, between them: *Über Homonymie und Homonyme im Deutschen*, pp. 64–66.

so lost must be replaced by others, since conflict arises between words that are in common use in the spoken language, that are, therefore, living, necessary elements in the vocabulary. The substitute word may come from the same language or dialect. Certain metaphorical terms are sometimes utilized in this way; *kabel*, the substitute word for *spicum* in the southwest of France, is probably such a term, as Gilliéron and Roques point out. It is a derivative of *kap, capo* 'head.' Thus *kabel* meant 'head (of wheat),' a use not unknown in other parts of France. Choice of synonyms may be made possible in various other ways within one dialect. *Pullus*, for example, probably was used in certain sections to mean the 'young cock.' Young fowls are in commercial demand. "Que le nom de la bête jeune, demandée le plus souvent, devienne l'appelation technique normale et relègue dans des acceptions plus ou moins péjoratives le nom primitif, qui ne donne aucune indication d'âge, c'est un fait dont la répétition sur divers points ne saurait nous étonner."[2] So, when the position of *gallus* was made precarious by homonymy, *pullus* was at hand to take its place and in this way became the only accepted form. In the same way the diminutive *kanot* (*cagnot*) replaced the form *ka(n* 'chien,' 'the adult dog' in southwest France, when the continued existence of the latter form was threatened because of its troublesome likeness to the name for the cat.[3]

The substitute word is, on the other hand, borrowed very frequently from another language or dialect. Such movements of words, "les voyages des mots" of Gilliéron and other writers on linguistic geography,[4] are not the result of chance. Words are borrowed in response to particular and definite needs in a language or dialect, and, in their "travels" from one area to another, they follow routes that are determined by particular geographical, historical, and social conditions in the history of peoples and languages, factors that are interactive and cannot be isolated.

In certain dialects of the south of France, for instance,[5] the need for an unambiguous term developed when, by normal phonological processes, the two Vulgar Latin forms *canis* 'dog' and *cattus* 'cat' lost the characteristics that served to differentiate them for a long period

2. Gilliéron and Roques, *Études de géographie linguistique*, p. 125.
3. See the immediately following paragraphs for further discussion and reference.
4. See Albert Dauzat, *La géographie linguistique* (Paris, 1922), pp. 151 ff.; Ernst Gamillscheg, *Die Sprachgeographie und ihre Ergebnisse für die allgemeine Sprachwissenschaft*, Neuphilologische Handbibliothek für die westeuropäischen Kulturen und Sprachen (Bielefeld and Leipzig, 1928), pp. 17 ff.; Jaberg, *Sprachgeographie*, pp. 9 ff.; and works of Gilliéron, in which the subject is treated in various connections.
5. The following example is taken from the work of A. Dauzat, based on the data of the *ALF*. He mentions it in *La géographie linguistique*, p. 68; he treats it at greater length in *Essais de géographie linguistique*, Nouvelle Série (Montpelier, Paris, 1938)¦ pp. 15–21.

of their history and became very much alike in sound. *Canis* became *chan* (then *chá*) in exactly those areas where *cattus* became *chat;* farther south, where palatalization of Latin *c, g* before *a* did not occur, *canis* became *can, cá,* while *cattus* became *cat.* The similarity of *chan, chá* to *chat,* and of *can, cá* to *cat,* and the even closer similarity of the plurals *chanz, chas* 'dogs' to *chaz* 'cats,' or *canz, cas* 'dogs' to *caz* 'cats,' would almost certainly give rise to troublesome ambiguity when the terms were used in rapid speech. For one of these conflicting terms a convenient substitute was at hand in the neighboring dialects—the forms *chin, chien* of those sections where *a* had been palatalized by a preceding palatal consonant. The original word for 'cat' remained; the borrowed terms for 'dog' spread gradually and steadily. Thus, in the present-day distribution of the form *chin* can be seen a striking instance of the "traveling of words." It spread from the neighborhood of Lyons, where it had developed by normal phonological processes, south along the Rhone valley and west along well-defined routes of travel; Lyons has been from early times an influential center for the distribution of word-forms because of its activity in trade and general intellectual development, and the Rhone valley has been a highway of communication particularly subject to influences from the north. The part played by mountainous sections, Le Massif Central in this case, as barriers to the movement of word-forms is also indicated in the chart showing the distribution of this form. Evidence that homonymic conflict occasioned the need for the borrowing of the new term becomes, if possible, still more surely certain when the investigation is pushed further. In areas in the extreme southwest and in Italy, where Vulgar Latin *cattus* became *gat,* the original term *kan* for 'dog' persisted; that is, in just those areas where confusion resulting from similarity in sound was rendered less likely, both of the traditional forms are common in the dialects of today.[6]

Thus the principle of homonymic conflict comes into close relationship with that other phase of linguistic geography, "les voyages des mots," and substitute words in instances of conflict may be of great significance, revealing the direction of language currents and the interrelation of language and social history.

The point of greatest consequence in this connection for the English language is the availability of French loan-words at most periods of its history, and of Scandinavian loan-words during certain more limited periods. From the Norman Conquest on, and for many years before 1066 as well, English has been a language rich in synonyms because of the strong influx into the native language of French words, through the Court and the "Oberschicht" of society, through the law-

6. See Dauzat, *La géographie linguistique,* p. 68.

courts, the church, trade relations. The Conquest, though probably the most powerful, was only one of the historical, political, and social factors bringing the influence of the French language into Britain. The Hundred Years' War and the political connections of the four-teenth century, the intellectual awakening in the late sixteenth cen-tury with its strong French element, the return of Charles II from the French court to the English throne—almost every century was marked by a fresh wave of French influence that had as its immediate result the enriching of the English vocabulary. For the same reasons, homonyms also have been frequent, and instances of conflict nu-merous. And if conflict has frequently been caused by a French im-portation colliding with an English homonym, it is also true that many French loan-words have served as substitutes for words weakened by homonymy and confusion arising from it, as in the case of *cover*, from Old French *cuvrir*, which generally replaced the native *heal*, from Old English *helan* 'to cover.'

Limitation of Words. Instead of complete loss, the limitation of particular words may result from collisions of homophones. A word may be restricted to one group or occupation, to one circle of inter-ests. *Weigh*, for example, is used in its former sense of 'to lift' only in the nautical phrase "to weigh anchor."[7] The jargon of ships and the sea has preserved many words lost, for different reasons, from the general vocabulary. *Ax, ex* 'axle,' in a similar way, is now a term limited to farming communities.[8] The restriction may be the more active process implied here, the actual narrowing of a word's sphere of use, or a more passive process, whereby a word is kept by the risk

7. See special study of *weigh* in this book.

8. *Ax(e, ex* 'axle,' from OE *æx-e, eax-e*, is not found, says the *NED*, after the Old English period except in compounds such as *ax-nail, ax-tree*. It is, however, a not uncommon term in the dialects of England and in the rural speech of certain parts of America. Wright records it (Joseph Wright, *The English Dialect Dictionary*, London, Oxford, New York, 1898. See *Ax*, sb.¹) in the dialects of Scotland, Northumberland, Northamptonshire, and a large group of counties in the South; he gives the pronun-ciations [aks, jaks, ɛks, jɛks]. It is recorded in the *Dictionary of American English on Historical Principles* (Chicago, 1938. Sir William Craigie and J. R. Hulbert, edi-tors) in the seventeenth-century compounds *ax-pin* and *ex-pin*. Notes on its present-day American use are given by Martha Jane Gibson: "Survival of Old English *Eax*, *Æx*," *American Speech*, x (1935), 155–6.

Though the fact that the form which eventually replaced this one in common speech, that is, *axle*, from ON *öxull* in *öxul-tre*, is not recorded before the thirteenth century and that *ax* 'axle' is not recorded except in very limited uses after the eleventh century makes it impossible to argue with certainty that the loss of the latter was occasioned by homonymic conflict, it is, nevertheless, quite probable that the likeness in sound of *ax* 'axle' to *ax* 'a hewing tool' caused the recession of *ax* 'axle' and led to the adoption of the longer ON term with the same meaning. It is particularly significant, in this connection, that the word in its continued existence through the centuries appears most frequently in compounds (*ax-pin, ax-tree, ax-nail*) and in forms with pronunciation differing from that of the more common *ax* 'hewing tool,' for example the *yax, yex, ix, ex* of various quotations.

of homonymy from spreading beyond a particular group.[9] Again, the narrowing in use of a word may be a semantic limitation. *Gate*, now spelled *gait*, once a fairly common term meaning 'road,' now exists in Standard English only in one sense, that of 'carriage, manner of going.' *Weigh* also has now, as a term in general use, a specific sense. Or the restriction may be purely syntactical. In phrases, words frequently live long after they have ceased to be used in common parlance. Such phrases are, in English, not infrequently alliterative, the alliteration serving still further to preserve the word: *tray* in *tray and teen*,[10] *weeds* in *widow's weeds*,[11] *tide* in *time and tide*.[12]

Changes in the Form of Words. Loss or limitation in use may result from conflict. A third possible consequence, change in form of one or more of the words concerned, has been demonstrated in numerous studies of the French vocabulary, where material in the *Atlas linguistique de la France* makes such demonstration possible and peculiarly convincing. Speakers may find it more convenient to use a variant form of an existing word than to borrow a new term, and, in response to the need for them, variants come into existence in numerous ways. This process of deterioration and building up of language, the formation of variants or the importation of forms more closely related to the original source to take the place of others not suitable, for various reasons, for general use, Gilliéron and others after him have called the pathology and therapeutics of words.[13]

A word threatened in its existence by some one of the vicissitudes of language development, as, for example, homonymic conflict, may

9. G. K. Zipf speaks of this "influence of the small speech-group in minimizing the risk of homonymy": *The Psycho-Biology of Language* (Boston, 1935), p. 30.

10. See special studies of *gate, weigh*, and *tray* in this book.

11. OE *wēod* 'weed' and OE *wǣd, wǣde* 'a garment' were not homonyms. Only in the 18th century, with the leveling of ME close and open ẹ and ẹ, did they finally become so. The chronology of the records of the two words does not offer conclusive evidence of conflict between them. Both words are recorded from Old English to modern times, and it is difficult to determine just when *weed* 'a garment' ceased to be used commonly and became archaic. It is quite possible that the subtle factor of fashion in words operated here, its connection with mourning possibly hastening its disuse in other connections. But it is also more than likely that possibility of collision with the more common *weed* 'a plant' was a strongly contributing factor in the restriction of *weed('s* 'garment('s' to the plural form and particularly to the alliterative phrase mentioned.

12. See Section iv of this chapter. Öhmann discusses the same aspect of the question—"Die erhaltende wirkung der redensarten bei homonymen," pp. 66–68 of his treatise on homonymy. He mentions, among other examples from German, the survival of *gift* 'gabe' in the phrase *gift und gabe.*

13. See Jules Gilliéron, *Pathologie et thérapeutique verbales, Collection linguistique publiée par la Société de Linguistique de Paris*, XI, Paris, 1921; particular studies by Gilliéron such as those in connection with the word *abeille*, to be mentioned later; general discussion by Dauzat, *La géographie linguistique*, pp. 83–95. Öhmann, without using the particular words *pathology*, etc., discusses in considerable detail such effects of homonymic interference on the German vocabulary: *Über Homonymie und Homonyme im Deutschen.*

be strengthened, made unambiguous by a modifying phrase or term that is in time considered almost an integral part of the word. *Pomme* in French has two meanings, *pomme de terre* means 'potato.' *Mouche* is a word meaning 'a fly' and, in dialects of the north of France, 'a swarm' and 'a hive'; *mouche à miel* means unmistakably a 'honey-bee.' The two adjectives *light* in English—*light* as opposed to 'heavy,' and *light* as opposed to 'dark'—might well cause confusion.[14] But compounds are with increasing frequency substituted for them, compounds that are immediately clear, unambiguous. The former adjective becomes *light-weight,* the latter *light-colored.* "Thus tailors speak of light-weight materials, and a man advertises 'a light-coloured gray overcoat' (NED's quotation), where of course 'light gray overcoat' would be ambiguous."[15] Instances are known in which the attributive word assumes the significance of the whole and so eliminates the possibility of confusion to which the original word is subject; *mouche d'essaim* becomes, for example, in the dialect of a particular section of northern France merely *essaim* 'bee'; that is, the qualifying word which in the beginning preserved the term *mouche* from ambiguity assumes the function of the whole phrase.[16]

"Agglutination,"[17] the process by which elements are added to the original form of the word, is a common phenomenon. Suffixes, modifying adjectives, prefixes and prefixed elements have all served at various times as differentiating elements. *Épinette, épine blanche, nobépine* with the *n* of the indefinite article, are dialectal terms in different parts of France for the white thorn, as opposed to other varieties of the thorn.[18] *Nep,* the dialectal word for 'wasp' in one locality in France, may be explained as an example of the absorption of the *n* of the indefinite article by the noun—here *ep*—the *n* giving

14. See Robert J. Menner, "The Conflict of Homonyms in English," *Language,* XII (1936), 229–44.

15. *Ibid.,* p. 242.

16. The word *essaim* (< L *exāmen*) meant originally 'swarm'; by folk-etymology, through association in the popular mind with the word *es* 'bee,' it came to mean regularly 'swarm of bees,' and through the process mentioned above simply 'bee' in particular areas. Thus its presence is due both to folk-etymology and to the exigencies of homonymic conflict, of which a full explanation is not possible here. See Jules Gilliéron, *Généalogie des mots qui désignent l'Abeille,* Paris, 1918; pages 35 and 44 in particular mention the reduction of *mouche d'essaim* to *essaim* 'bee.'

The same process of reduction, though not as the result of homonymic conflict, is to be observed in English. A Toledo blade is frequently called a Toledo, Calico cloth is commonly calico; in American parlance a Winchester rifle becomes simply a Winchester, a forty-four calibre shotgun is a forty-four, a Panama hat a Panama. The English word *planet* is derived ultimately from the Greek ἀστέρες πλανῆται 'wandering stars,' that is, from the original modifying term. Gilliéron cites also, from French, *champagne* from *vin de Champagne, une* (automobile) *Renaut, un* (aéroplane) *Blériot,* etc.: *L'Abeille,* pp. 35, 44.

17. Dauzat, *La géographie linguistique,* pp. 80–81.

18. Jaberg, *Sprachgeographie,* pp. 22 ff.

the word renewed vitality in its conflict with similar forms for 'bee.'[19] The English vocabulary offers examples of corresponding processes. *Pail* 'a vessel for carrying water, milk, etc.' is found in documents as early as the fourteenth century, and is probably derived from OE *pæȝel* (< VL *pagella*), perhaps influenced by OF *paielle*.[20] *Pale* (*NED*, sb.[1]), from French *pal* 'a stake,' was taken into English in the same century. The presence of these two words probably accounts for the failure of *pale*, related to French *pale* 'spade, shovel, blade,' to find a permanent place in English, while the diminutive forms of the latter, *pallet* 'a wooden instrument consisting of a flat blade, with handle attached, used by potters and others in shaping their work,' and *pallet, palette* 'a flat thin tablet of wood or porcelain used by artists for mixing colors' both are terms found commonly in English, though limited to some extent to the vocabularies of potters, artists, etc.[21] The diminutive, being differentiated in form from *pale* 'a shovel,' and not so liable to semantic confusion with the homonymous *pallet* 'a straw bed' as *pale* 'a shovel' would have been with its homonyms meaning 'bucket' and 'stake,' remained in the language; the term from which it was derived is used today only in a highly specialized sense. The *n-* of *near* 'kidney' also, it is probable, acted as a protecting agent when *near, ear* 'kidney' came into conflict with *ear* 'organ of hearing.'[22]

Real contaminations, etymologically speaking, sometimes become the accepted forms of words, as did *weps* for *wes* 'wasp' when the latter came into conflict with *wes* 'bee,' in the Walloon dialect.[23] The study of folk-etymology is, here again, linked to that of homonymy of words, for the form which arises from a mistaken conception of the origin of a word sometimes succeeds in maintaining that word in a language or patois from which it has disappeared in its original form.

Both dialects and standard language not infrequently have recourse to borrowing, or sometimes reborrowing, in their unconscious efforts to avoid difficult situations and ambiguities of expression. Dialects, for various reasons, draw upon the word-resources of the

---

19. Gilliéron, *L'Abeille*, p. 206.

20. See F. Holthausen, *Altenglisches etymologisches Wörterbuch* (Heidelberg, 1934), under *pæȝel;* M. S. Serjeantson, *A History of Foreign Words in English* (London, 1935), pp. 16, 50, 279; and the *NED*, where particular reference is made to the possible connection of the word with OF *paielle*.

21. *Pallet* and *palette* are merely differing forms of the same word in its different senses and applications. The latter form, *palette*, is becoming fixed as the spelling for the artist's color-board; *pallet* is the usual form for the potter's board. As the two become more and more distinct, even to being thought of as two separate words, confusion between them may lead to inconvenience. At present, the two are kept distinct by the milieu in which each is used.

22. See special study following.   23. Gilliéron, *L'Abeille*, pp. 137 ff.

standard language; the Walloon dialect took the term *ep* from French when a new word was needed for 'bee.'[24] The standard language, in its turn, may borrow from its root languages; Gilliéron has shown how French replaced *esmer*, which by normal development would have become homonymous with *aimer*, with *estimer*, a form more closely akin to its Latin source.[25]

When homonymic conflict makes it necessary or desirable that substitute terms be found for words likely to be mutually confused, such means of differentiation, these "moyens thérapeutiques,"[26] are not infrequently utilized, and the variants—the diminutives, the contaminations, the borrowings or reborrowings, etc.—thus become the only accepted terms.[27] Gilliéron's figurative terminology, "pathology and therapeutics of words," unless one stresses constantly the unconscious nature of the various processes, is likely to be misleading; but the idea involved is a sound one. Words liable to disuse because of confusion are removed from the sphere of conflict by only slight differentiation of form and are sometimes thus given renewed vitality.

iii. Objections to the Theory of Homonymic Conflict

The conflict of homonyms has exerted a demonstrable influence on the vocabulary of certain given languages—French, for example, German, English. It has caused the loss of some words, the limitation in use and change in form of others. But there are certain phenomena of language, certain homonyms in the ordinary English vocabulary, for example, that seem to argue against the validity of the theory. The very richness of homonyms in the present-day English vocabulary has been urged as evidence to discount the theory.[1] Many such arguments may be disregarded, the writers having failed to observe the fundamental requirements of the theory—phonetic identity of

24. Gilliéron, *L'Abeille*, p. 136.
25. *Ibid.*, pp. 267 ff. See also Dauzat, *La géographie linguistique*, p. 87.
26. See Gilliéron, *L'Abeille*, p. 138, where the expression "moyen thérapeutique" is used.
27. For a detailed study of the kind see Gilliéron, *L'Abeille*. The section, pp. 135 ff., "Conséquences de la Confusion de 'guêpe' avec 'abeille,'" offers a succinct demonstration of the significance of his phrase, "la thérapeutique des mots."
1. Sir Robert Bridges, *On English Homophones*, p. 24, takes account of this possibility: "For the contrary contention, namely, that homophones do not destroy themselves, there is prima facie evidence in the long list of survivors, and in the fact that a vast number of words which have not this disadvantage are equally gone out of use." Holthausen also mentions the objection: "Vom Aussterben der Wörter," *Germanisch-Romanische Monatsschrift*, VII (1915–19), 196. He writes: "Lautlicher Zusammenfall z.B. braucht noch lange nicht den Tod eines Wortes herbeizuführen, da ja alle Sprachen viele Homonyma besitzen, die fröhlich mit- und nebeneinander leben." He is at the moment referring to Teichert's argument that homonymy may cause the loss of a word only when there is a synonym at hand to take its place: F. Teichert, *Über das Aussterben alter Wörter im Verlaufe der englischen Sprachgeschichte* (Erlangen, 1912), pp. 47–8.

the words concerned, similar syntactical functions, use within the same sphere of ideas. Miss Richter's example from French, in her essay on homonymy, is such an instance.[2] She shows that *l'imiter* and *limiter* are to be differentiated by the varying intonation, sentence-melody, of the sentences in which they might be used and implies that for reasons similar to this there can be few instances of conflict of homonyms. Her contention in the case of the two words quoted is probably true. There are undoubtedly other words, too, that would be kept distinct by the factors of accent and intonation. But the terms *imiter* and *limiter* are not, in the first place, well within the compass of the theory: they are not closely placed within the same sphere of ideas, and would be differentiated in any case by context. Though her objection is one to be considered carefully and remembered at all times in such investigations, it remains true that there are words used in so nearly the same way that they would receive the same accent and intonation in sentences and as a result would be the cause of confusion. Many of the homonyms listed by Sir Robert Bridges, who writes from a different point of view, are, likewise, not subject to confusion and may not be used in support of his too extravagant assertion that "Homophones are a nuisance": many are different parts of speech, as, for example, *bee* and *be, arch* (sb.) and *arch* (adj.), *count* (sb.) and *count* (v.); still more are, individually, in very different circles of thought—*case* 'event' and *case* 'receptacle,' *cape* 'dress' and *cape* 'headland,' *gum* 'resin' and *gum* 'of the teeth.'[3]

But there remain certain examples of words, persisting in spite of homonymy and used in closely similar circumstances, that cannot be so easily accounted for. Such are *raze* 'to demolish' and *raise* 'to lift up'; *right* (sb.) and *rite*, perhaps, at one period of their history;[4] the verbs *sow* and *sew*, and *baste* 'to sew together loosely' and *baste* 'to moisten (a roasting joint).' Differentiation in spelling, as in *right* and *rite*, may serve, to some small extent, to keep such terms apart, especially when one or both of them is more likely to be found in the vocabulary of the lettered classes.[5] It is quite possible that *raze* is

2. Elise Richter, *Über Homonymie*, in *Festschrift für . . . Paul Kretschmer* (Vienna, Leipzig, New York, 1926), p. 171.

3. Sir Robert Bridges, *On English Homophones*.

4. See Otto Jespersen, *A Modern English Grammar on Historical Principles* (1st ed., Heidelberg, 1909), 1, 285, § 10.14: "*right = rite* (often confused in EE, especially in *rights of love = rites of love*)." But he adds, "Some of these were so little used (*mite, rite* . . .) that mistakes could not be very frequent."

5. This view has been held by several writers on the subject of homonyms. H. Bradley writes: "We have seen that one notable weakness of spoken English is the multitude of words that are pronounced alike but differ in meaning. The partial freedom of the written language from this fault is in itself a good thing; but it tends to perpetuate the evil by rendering it more tolerable. With educated people, the utterance of a word is usually accompanied by some obscure reminiscence of its spelling; their notion of the word is a blend of its audible and its visible form. Hence, when two

even now gradually losing ground before the more frequently used *raise*. *Sow* and *sew* present little real difficulty, for the syntactical constructions in which each usually occurs, the words and ideas frequently associated with them, differentiate them clearly. "Sow the fields with grain," "Sow the wind and reap the whirlwind," "The birds . . . who neither sow nor reap," "For a late summer and autumn crop, sow in the end of February": the sense is invariably clear. The same is true of *sew* 'to fasten with thread': "tents of . . . buffalo skins, sewed together and stretched on long poles," "She sat steadily at her work, sewing away at the shirts," "Will you sew up this rent for me?" "She is sewing with too long a thread." Though both words are common among the same groups of people, the very fact that one pertains to work in the fields, the other to indoor pursuits would tend to keep them apart. Contextual connections do so very clearly. *Baste* 'to sew together loosely' and *baste* 'to moisten (a roasting joint)' are somewhat more difficult. Both are "indoor" words, used by the same person, possibly, within the same hour. Actual confusion has indeed been caused by them, when one or the other is an unfamiliar word to the hearer. But they are not likely to be confused in ordinary speech, again because of the context and the syntactical constructions usual to each. "Baste the hem up," "Roast the chicken slowly, basting it occasionally," "Baste it with its own gravy," "She basted the seams quickly": only rarely, if at all, would there be possibility of real confusion.

B. Trnka in his article on homonymy finds this an important aspect of the study of English homonyms. English with its tendency toward monosyllabism and its complex vocabulary has many homophones, but he believes that the English-speaking person is seldom at a loss in using them, because it is his habit to associate meanings with words according to their sentence-connections.[6] Context and

words of the same sound happen to be distinguished in spelling, we are often imperfectly conscious of their identity to the ear. . . . Now oral language, when the influence of writing does not interfere, shows a tendency to free itself from such homophones as often cause inconvenience": see *Spoken and Written English*, in *The Collected Papers of Henry Bradley* (Oxford, 1928), pp. 183–4. Among others, Öhmann considers the question in his work on homonyms (see Einleitung and pp. 53 ff.). E. Branys, who refers to Bradley, mentions it: *Homonyme Substantive im Neuenglischen* (Berlin dissertation, 1938), pp. 10 ff.

6. B. Trnka, "Bemerkungen zur Homonymie," *Travaux du Cercle Linguistique de Prague*, IV (1931), 154: "Im ersten Falle [i.e., words that are homonyms in all associated forms] kann die von dem Sprechenden gemeinte Bedeutung des Homonyms aus dem semasiologischen Zusammenhang erfasst werden. Im zweiten Falle [i.e., words that are not homonymous in all forms] ist die von dem Sprechenden gemeinte Bedeutung nicht nur aus dem Zusammenhang, sondern regelmässig auch aus der syntaktischen Verbindung ersichtlich . . ." and "Der Englischsprechende ist viel mehr als ein Čechischsprechender geneigt, dieselbe Lautkombination je nach dem Wortzusammenhang im Satze mit verschiedenen Bedeutungen zu assoziieren, und die

syntactical constructions are of basic importance in any consideration of the effects of homonymy in English.

Objections like these, however, emphasize two points that the proponent of the theory of homonymic conflict must keep constantly in mind. The processes of language are seldom quick-moving or instantaneous. The loss of words, in particular, is a slow process, for it is the nature of words to live, to persist in a language. Seldom would a word be completely lost, once it was established in a language or dialect, in less than two or three generations of speakers. Frequently the disappearance is even more gradual. Each instance of conflict involves a separate study; only in rather general ways may several be grouped together. And in each case there are particular factors that affect the rate at which words disappear. In general, the process is a slow one. "Jahrhundertelang," says Jaberg, "dauert meist der Kampf zwischen zwei sprachlichen Typen."[7]

And, on the negative side, the student of the theory must always remember that the conflict of homonyms is only one of many reasons for the disappearance of words. It is quite possible that two or more factors may be involved in the loss of a single word. Frequently the loss of words that, at first glance, seem to illustrate the theory, can be accounted for on quite other grounds, and accounted for thus with far greater probability. A casual glance may seem to discover in the disappearance (exc. hist. and dial.) of *crowd* 'a musical instrument' an instance of conflict with *crowd* (of people). A 1622 quotation from Middleton runs: "Enter Fiddlers and others. Evander. Stay the crowd awhile." *Crowd*, in this sentence, means 'a musical instrument.'[8] Confusion with the homonym seems possible. But it is far more likely that fashion alone was responsible for the disuse of the word. New instruments, violins for example, replaced the older ones, and brought new names with them. *Flask*, from French, replaced English **flash*, from OE *flasce*, after the sixteenth century not, probably, because **flash* 'a bottle' conflicted with *flash* 'a pool, marshy place' or *flash* 'burst of light,' but because new utensils came in and were found superior to old ones. The American *duster* 'light coat' disappeared when the closed automobile became usual, not because of homonymic conflict with *duster* 'a dusting implement.' Because they are often closely connected with the question of homonymic conflict and its effects, and because they must never be lost sight of in studies of the subject, some other causes of the loss of words are touched upon in the following section.

Gefahr der Homonymie war nie ein Hindernis, ein gleichlautendes fremdes Wort zu entlehnen." Erika Branys, also, in her discussion of homonyms in present-day English, p. 87, states this as an important item of consideration.

7. Jaberg, *Sprachgeographie*, p. 11.   8. See *NED*, under *Crowd*, sb.¹ b.

iv. Other Causes of the Loss of Words

Quite generally the reasons for the change and loss of words have been grouped by writers on the subject under two heads—cultural causes and purely linguistic causes, Jaeschke's "Kulturgeschichtliche Bedingungen" and "Sprachliche Bedingungen,"[1] that is, forces that lie outside the words themselves and others that are implicit in their form, sound, or meaning. The two can never be entirely dissociated.

In the one group are all those events and forces that have influenced, directly and indirectly, the life of a people at various periods in its history and have left traces on the language of that people. Such are wars and invasions, innovations in religion and ecclesiastical procedure, in law and medicine and science, in education and learning, in the fields of art and architecture, changes in the ordinary life of the home and its equipment, changes in fashion, changing ideas or systems in all fields of thought. Many words have entered the English language as the direct result of such factors as these. Some were additions; others supplanted words of longer standing in the language, the old words losing favor among speakers for one reason or another, the new ones taking their places.

Many Old English forms, for example, were replaced by others drawn from the languages of the Scandinavian invaders of Britain in the eighth and ninth centuries: OE *ǣ* 'law' ceased to be used, *law* (< ON *lagu*) took its place; English *lyft* 'sky' was gradually restricted to dialectal use, where it is still found today, and was replaced by *sky* (< ON *sky*); *egg* (< ON *egg*) supplanted the native *ey* (< OE *ǣg*). Countless other Modern English words date from the time of the Norman invasion, that strengthened the already vigorous importation of French words into England and shifted, in large part, the "Oberschicht" of society, thus occasioning many changes not only in the way of life of most groups in the country but also in their speech.[2] New methods of worship brought the French word *ure*,

1. Kurt Jaeschke, *Beiträge zur Frage des Wortschwundes im Englischen, Sprache und Kultur der germanischen und romanischen Völker*, Anglistische Reihe, VI, Breslau, 1931. See Table of Contents. For other discussions of this general subject see Gamillscheg, *Die Sprachgeographie*, pp. 46–52; Emil Hemken, *Das Aussterben alter Substantiva im Verlaufe der englischen Sprachgeschichte*, Kiel, 1906; Wilhelm Oberdörffer, *Das Aussterben altenglischer Adjektive und ihr Ersatz im Verlaufe der englischen Sprachgeschichte*, Kiel, 1908; Johannes Offe, *Das Aussterben alter Verba und ihr Ersatz im Verlaufe der englischen Sprachgeschichte*, Kiel, 1908; Friedrich Teichert, *Über das Aussterben alter Wörter im Verlaufe der englischen Sprachgeschichte*, Erlangen, 1912; Robert Feist, *Studien zur Rezeption des französischen Wortschatzes im Mittelenglischen, Beiträge zur englischen Philologie*, XXV, Leipzig, 1934; and others listed in the bibliography at the end of this work.
2. H. Naumann, "Über das sprachliche Verhältnis von Ober- zu Unterschicht," *Jahrbuch für Philologie* (later, *Idealistische Philologie*), I (1925), 55–69, gives a discussion of this aspect of the development of language.

hure, AF *houre* (< Lat. *hōra*), which was quickly extended in use and finally replaced the native *tīd* and *stund* in ordinary speech.[3] *Judgment* (< F *jugement*) restricted the use of the English *dōm*, MnE *doom* to particular connotations; *physician* (< OF *fisician* < Lat. *physic-a*) replaced OE *lǣce*, MnE *leech*, in most uses; *astrologer* (< F *astrologie*, with addition of *er*) supplanted the native terms *tunglere* and *tīdscēawere*.[4] OE *þēodend* and *wendere* were replaced by *translator* and *interpreter*, both of French origin.[5] Architecture (OE *weallīm* replaced by *mortar* < OF *mortier*, and later *cement* < OF *ciment*);[6] ordinary daily life (OE *þorp*, now archaic or historical, replaced by *village* < OF *village*);[7] fashions (French-derived *attire, array, apparel* appearing in the fourteenth century, OE *tyslung* vanishing):[8] all aspects of life and all periods of history offer examples of the loss of words under the impact of changing forces in the social life.

Less easily defined, but probably one of the most powerful causes of the loss of words, is the influence of fashion, in the broader meaning of the term. This, in a sense, lies midway between the two groups here being discussed, the sociological and the phonological-morphological causes of loss of words. A word becomes unpopular for various reasons, some obvious, others involving less definable currents of fashion, of interests, of fads even, cultural influences that are frequently obscure and devious. Because one word is thought of as more "elegant" or more "correct" than another, it is preferred; and the unpopular words may fall into disuse and even eventually disappear. At present, *ill* is, for reasons not altogether clear,[9] preferred as more "elegant" than *sick*, particularly in cultured British speech; *sick* is becoming more and more restricted in meaning. The verb *tote* 'to carry,' in current use in the United States in the seventeenth century, is now a colloquialism, found chiefly in the South and New England, and, more generally, in such slang phrases as "to tote a gun"; in the South it is in definite disfavor as a word limited to the vocabulary of the uneducated.

In the second group of causes, those that are implicit in the words themselves, are loss of affix-syllables and too great shortening of a

---

3. *Hour* appears in English first in the canonical sense (1225, *Ancren Riwle*), according to the *NED*. The strictly temporal senses, however, appear soon afterward. See also Feist, *Studien zur Rezeption des französischen Wortschatzes im Mittelenglischen*, pp. 29–30.

Stound (< OE *stund*) is found in English dialect today; *tide* (< OE *tīd* 'time, hour') still lives, chiefly in phrases and combinations such as "Time and tide wait for no man," *noon-tide, eventide, Lammas-tide. Tide* 'of the sea,' originally the same word, has probably an independent history: see *NED*.

4. Jaeschke, *Beiträge*, p. 29.
6. *Ibid.*, p. 31.   7. *Ibid.*, p. 95.

5. *Ibid.*, p. 28.
8. *Ibid.*, p. 36.

9. It is possible that the influence of the word *seasick* has been strong enough to affect the simple term *sick*.

word in consequence, difficult pronunciation, possible homonymy, the effect of euphemisms on language, isolation of words in form or meaning, etc.

Teichert and others, not very convincingly, attribute the loss of a number of words to their being short, or so lacking in "Lautgehalt" that they lose effectiveness. OE *not*, he says, yielded place to the stronger synonyms, "den kräftigeren Synonymen," *mark, sign.* He finds OE *mitta* inconveniently slight in comparison with French *measure;* OE *gener, ner* with *refuge, safety;* OE *genip* with *mist, gloom, darkness.*[10] Oberdörffer thinks it probable that *cāf*, because of shortness, "wegen seiner kurzen Lautgestalt," was replaced by *prompt.*[11] Gamillscheg, referring to Gilliéron, agrees with him that "die Reduzierung des Wortkörpers einer Bezeichnung auf einen einzigen Vokal die Ursache zum Wortuntergang sein kann." He adds, "Zweifellos sucht die Sprache diesen 'mutilés phonétiques' einen stärkeren Wortkörper zu geben." As an example he gives Old French *hui*, that exists today only in *aujourd'hui.*[12] The express passage in Gilliéron's work to which he refers is a note in the work on *abeille.*[13] Other parts of that work seem to contradict the implication that the mere fact of phonetic reduction proves detrimental to a word, and so do numerous common terms in English.[14] Such arguments need further proof, if they are to be accepted. Jespersen looks upon the gradual development in English of a strong tendency toward monosyllabism not "as decay from a more developed to a more primitive type" of language, in which light it was formerly regarded, but as "a progressive tendency towards a more perfect structure."[15] He finds a purpose in the shortness of some words,[16] their very shortness adding to their effectiveness under particular circumstances. His discussion, chiefly concerned though it is with other aspects of the development of language, argues implicitly against the unconsidered assumption of this principle—that mere shortness, or lack of "fullness" in sound, may be the reason for the disappearance of words. It is enough to say that as a contributing factor phonetic "mutilation"

10. Teichert, *Über das Aussterben alter Wörter*, pp. 30–1.

11. Oberdörffer, *Das Aussterben altenglischer Adjektive*, p. 10. See also Jaeschke, *Beiträge*, pp. 41–2.

12. Gamillscheg, *Die Sprachgeographie*, p. 51.

13. Gilliéron, *L'Abeille*, p. 38, note 2: "Officiellement: Ault (ȯlt). Pour éviter la mutilation phonétique en ȯ, les indigènes appellent leur village Burkèdaw (= Bourg d'Ault) comme ils appellent VILLE D'EU et non EU la ville la plus rapprochée."

14 For example, *e* 'bee' continues to live in certain localities of France. In English, *go* represents an earlier *gān*, *sit* an earlier *sittan*, *laugh* earlier *hliehhan*.

15. O. Jespersen, *Monosyllabism in English*, in *Linguistica* (Copenhagen, London, 1933), p. 384. "Monosyllables constitute the most indispensable part of the English vocabulary and are with few exceptions those words which the small child learns first," he writes in another place (p. 386).

16. Jespersen, *Monosyllabism in English*, p. 408: "In other cases we see that the very shortness or length of words is utilized for purposes of expressiveness. . . ."

may operate to cause the loss of a word; it may, for instance, cause it to lose its identity through confusion with homonyms, or through isolation in form or meaning. Shortness, or phonetic slightness, in and of itself, is not likely to occasion the loss of many words.

A difficult pronunciation may bring about the disuse of a term, when there are more euphonious synonyms at hand. Offe lists several Old English words that probably owed their loss of status to this factor: *hlēoþorian* (or *hlēoðrian*), replaced by *shout*, etc.; *drysmian* 'to become gloomy,' with its difficult preterite forms.[17] Teichert[18] and Oberdörffer[19] offer similar instances. Jaeschke discusses a number of instances from the Old English vocabulary, noting especially those with initial *þw-*.[20]

Euphemism is an active factor in the development of vocabulary. People tend always in polite speech to avoid terms of unpleasant connotation, and such terms gradually become vulgarisms or archaisms, or are lost altogether. *Harlot,* in English, is by way of becoming archaic or purely literary, being superseded by *prostitute.* It was itself, probably, a euphemism for synonymous words.[21] Numerous other examples are given by writers on the subject of word-loss.[22] It is enough, indeed, that a word sound like one of unpleasant connotation for its existence to be threatened. An example in French is to be found in Jaberg's study of the word *lapin.*[23] The classic example in English is perhaps the word *ass,* now seldom heard in ordinary polite speech, especially in America, but maintained still in the literary language through the influence of Biblical passages.[24]

The position of words may be undermined by their becoming isolated from others of the same family, as the result of different phonetic development or of previous loss of related words; by false association

17. Offe, *Das Aussterben alter Verba,* pp. 13–14.

18. Teichert, *Über das Aussterben alter Wörter,* pp. 33–5.

19. Oberdörffer, *Das Aussterben altenglischer Adjektive,* p. 13.

20. Jaeschke, *Beiträge,* pp. 38–41.

21. Cf. *NED,* under *Harlot,* sb. 5. c.: "(Very frequent in 16th c. Bible versions, where Wyclif had *hoore,* whore; prob. as a less offensive word.)"

22. Hemken, p. 37; Offe, pp. 36–8; Oberdörffer, pp. 20–1; Teichert, pp. 52 ff.; Jaeschke, pp. 73 ff.

23. See Chapter I, Section i, note 7, of this work.

24. *NED,* see *Ass:* "(In familiar use, the name *ass* is now to a great extent superseded by *donkey* (in Scotland *cuddie*); but *ass* is always used in the language of Scripture, Natural History, proverb, and fable; also, in ordinary use, in Ireland.)". Bloomfield refers to the same phenomenon (*Language,* p. 396): ". . . in both languages this word [i.e., one for 'rabbit'] died out because it resembled a word that was under a tabu of indecency. For the same reason, *rooster* and *donkey* are replacing *cock* and *ass* in American English. In such cases there is little real ambiguity, but some hearers react nevertheless to the powerful stimulus of the tabu-word; having called forth ridicule or embarrassment, the speaker avoids the innocent homonym. It is a remarkable fact that the tabu-word itself has a much tougher life than the harmless homonym." The expression "Don't be a jack-ass" is an evasion, at times preferred by some persons, of the unwelcome association of the word *ass.*

with words similar in form or sound; by lack of appropriateness to the sense-content; by other circumstances that have been discussed by various writers.[25] All such influences in the development of a vocabulary must be treated with the utmost circumspection, with attention to the facts of chronology and distribution that are furnished in dictionaries, atlases, glossaries, and with the idea constantly uppermost that each word has its own individuality and its own history, closely related and interrelated though that must be with the history of other words, that the reasons for the obsolescence of words will vary as the words themselves vary.[26] Generalizations can be made only on the basis of detailed study of many individual cases.

The conflict of homonyms is thus only one of many alleged causes of the loss of words, and one of the least frequent in comparison with the vast number of words lost in English. It has played an unmistakable part in the development of the French and English vocabularies, a somewhat smaller part, probably, in the evolution of the German because the phonetic changes in German since Old High German times have been comparatively few; but the student of the subject cannot be too careful in his consideration of all the possible reasons for the disappearance of words. He must remember that frequently several causes operate together. A word, for example, may be given up because there is another more suitable in sound to the idea it conveys, and preferred as well among members of the classes who often control fashion in words. The native English names for nobles and ranks of nobility gave way before French terms after the Conquest because they were no longer needed and also, probably, because they were looked upon as belonging to the vocabulary of classes inferior to the French court circles. Seldom are circumstances so simple and obvious that we may say, without possibility of debate, that one cause alone was responsible for the loss of a word. The most that we can say is that homonymy, for example, was a contributing factor, in some cases almost certainly the main factor, causing the unpopularity of certain terms and the disappearance of others.

25. See Hemken, Oberdörffer, Offe, Teichert, Jaeschke's *Beiträge,* Holthausen's "Vom Aussterben der Wörter," Gamillscheg's *Die Sprachgeographie,* and others listed in the bibliography.

26. This idea has been emphasized by many writers on linguistic geography. "Die Sprachgeographie hat . . . die Tatsache besonders hervortreten lassen, dass jedes Wort seine eigene Geschichte hat, ebenso was seine lautliche wie seine Bedeutungsentwicklung betrifft," writes Gamillscheg (*Die Sprachgeographie,* p. 10). Jaberg (*Sprachgeographie,* p. 6) says much the same: "In Wirklichkeit hat jedes Wort seine besondere Geschichte." It was a basic idea in the work of Gilliéron; Jaberg writes of him, "Si la géographie linguistique, en Allemagne, tend à la synthèse et cherche à sortir du domaine de la linguistique pure, Gilliéron, lui, a été dominé par cette idée que chaque élément linguistique a son histoire individuelle, histoire qu'il faut d'abord établir consciencieusement et dans tous ses détails, avant de songer à des synthèses. . . ." (*Aspects géographiques du langage, Société de Publications Romanes et Françaises,* XVIII [Paris, 1936], p. 13.)

II

History of the Theory in France and Elsewhere

THE theory of the conflict of homonyms thus forms one part of the comparatively new branch of general linguistic science, so-called linguistic geography.[1] It developed directly out of studies of material in the *Atlas linguistique de la France*. When Gilliéron and other students of the *Atlas* began to realize the full significance of the geographical and social distribution of words and word-forms throughout France and to seek, by means of studies of particular words, the various causes that might account for it, they discovered the facts that led to the formulation of the theory. They found that words have disappeared in just those areas where homonymy with other words capable of being confused with them developed; that these same words existed together for centuries in other areas, often adjacent, where such homonymy did not normally develop; that, when one such word in its homonymous form disappeared, related but phonetically differentiated forms frequently continued to exist:[2] such observations of the actual distribution of dialectal forms in France led to the formulation of the theory of homonymic conflict, as it has been outlined here.

The most important single writer on the subject of linguistic geography and its subdivision, the conflict of homonyms, was Jules Gilliéron. His conception of the plan for the *Atlas linguistique de la France* and his work in carrying it through to completion, and his subsequent interpretations of some of the charts composing that work mark the founding of the new "school." His earliest investigation of this kind to be published was that of the dialectal forms for SCIER in the south of France, SCIER *dans le Gaule Romane du Sud et de l'Est*.[3] It was written in collaboration with J. Mongin and published

1. A discussion of linguistic geography in general can be found in a number of books and articles written for the purpose of making clear the general outlines of the science. See, for example, Dauzat, *La géographie linguistique;* Gamillscheg, *Die Sprachgeographie;* Frings, "Sprachgeographie und Kulturgeographie," *Zeitschrift für Deutschkunde,* XLIV (1930), 546–62; Jaberg, "Die neuere Forschung auf dem Gebiete der romanischen Sprachgeographie," *Die Geisteswissenschaften,* XVIII (1914), 488–93; I. Iordan and J. Orr, *An Introduction to Romance Linguistics* (London, 1937), chap. 3. A good bibliography is given by Josef Schrijnen, in *Essai de bibliographie de géographie linguistique générale, Publications de la Commission d'Enquête Linguistique,* II, Nimègue, 1933.

2. For example, the derivatives of the feminine *gallina* persisted in the section where masculine *gat* (< *gallus*), homonymous with *gat* (< *cattus*), disappeared. This and other examples have been given in preceding sections.

3. J. Gilliéron and J. Mongin, *Étude de géographie linguistique.* SCIER *dans la Gaule Romane du Sud et de l'Est,* Paris, 1905.

in 1905. Not a long study,[4] it is nevertheless an important one in the history of the new methods of language study, as Dauzat says, "une petite étude qui prit la valeur d'un manifeste."[5] It illustrates several aspects of linguistic geography and demonstrates clearly the relation of homonymy to the shifting of terms.[6] Though the theory of homonymic conflict appeared in this work full-grown, clear in all its outlines, more demonstration was necessary before it could be accepted as a principle of language development. This followed shortly. Between 1905 and 1910, Gilliéron, again in collaboration, this time with Mongin and Mario Roques, published a series of articles[7] based on material in the *Atlas linguistique*, which were published in book form in 1912.[8] Two entire sections are devoted to "Mots en Collision,"[9] one of which is a study of *épi* and *épine* and the other the much-cited example of *gallus-cattus* in Gascony.[10] In 1912 Gilliéron alone published his work on the word *clavellus*,[11] and in 1918 the very significant and important study of terms denoting the bee in northern France, *Généalogie des mots qui désignent l'Abeille*. In both works, as in all those preceding, he demonstrates the significance in the history of words of possible conflict with other words homonymous with them and susceptible to mutual confusion.[12] In 1921 appeared his work *Pathologie et thérapeutique verbales*, devoted primarily, as the title shows, to the development of his belief that a language has at its command certain remedial measures when word-forms deteriorate and are in danger of extinction; homonymy is mentioned more than once as a possible destructive or disturbing

4. Thirty pages and five maps.   5. Dauzat, *La géographie linguistique*, p. 21.

6. In brief, the study shows that *serrare* 'scier' does not appear in particular areas in southern France because in those areas a homonym, *serare* 'fermer,' was in use and the two words were incompatible. The authors write (*op. cit.*, p. 8): ". . . nous attribuons la disparition de *serrare-scier*, et nous ne voyons pas d'autre explication possible, au malaise linguistique causé par la confusion réalisée ou toujours imminente de *sĕrrare-scier* et de *sĕrare-fermer.*"

7. In the *Revue de philologie française et de littérature*, Vols. xx–xxiv.

8. Gilliéron and Roques, *Études de géographie linguistique, d'après L'Atlas linguistique de la France*, Paris, 1912.

9. Cf. *Table des Matières.*

10. Other sections too are concerned with the question of homonymic conflict, notably that of *traire*, *mulgere*, and *molere*: Gilliéron and Roques, *Études de géographie linguistique*, pp. 10 ff.

11. *L'Aire* CLAVELLUS *d'après L'Atlas linguistique de la France*, Neuveville, 1912.

12. In *L'Aire* CLAVELLUS, he shows how derivatives of *clavus* 'nail' and *clavis* 'key' collided in the south of France, with resulting loss of the former and substitution for it of the diminutive form *clavellus;* in the north both persist, because there the original forms remained distinct as *clou* and *clef*, and so never conflicted.

In *L'Abeille* he shows, for example, how terms for 'bee' and for 'bird' came into conflict in one area; how, in another vicinity, designations of the bee and the wasp collided. Frequently in the course of his detailed, careful analysis of the situation he refers to minor instances (minor, that is, in relation to the immediate study) of evident conflict: *ep* 'abeille' with *ep* 'hache,' *ep* 'abeille' with *nep* 'nèfle' (*L'Abeille*, p. 138), *myel* 'merle' and *myel* 'miel' (*L'Abeille*, p. 76), etc.

force in the life of words.[13] Gilliéron's assumptions in regard to the theory of homonymic conflict have been criticized as being exaggerated and uncompromising at times; but his work alone was sufficient to establish the soundness of the theory as a means of explaining the disappearance of many words and the distribution of others.

His work was supplemented and supported further by a number of books and studies by his students and immediate followers. Mongin and Roques, already referred to, wrote in collaboration with Gilliéron. As early as 1908, Karl Jaberg, of the University of Bern, writing on the French vocabulary and drawing his materials of investigation from the *ALF*, published a series of studies which he entitled *Sprachgeographie*.[14] Very briefly he sketches some of the principal features of linguistic geography, homonymic conflict among them, illustrating each with detailed studies of particular words. Other works followed this, general discussions of linguistic geography and studies of particular terms such as his *Sprachgeographische Untersuchungen* (1908)[15] and the recent *Wie der Hundedachs zum Dachs und der Dachs zum Iltis Wird*.[16] His numerous works, in particular the monumental *Sprach- und Sachatlas Italiens und der Südschweig*, compiled and published (in part) in collaboration with Jacob Jud, have made his name outstanding among proponents of linguistic geography and the new linguistic methods implied in that term. In his recent *Aspects géographiques du langage*,[17] studies of the material of the Swiss and Italian atlas, the principle of homonymic conflict, though not prominent, has a place. In 1921 Albert Dauzat published his first series of studies in linguistic geography, *Essais de géographie linguistique: Noms d'animaux*, in which he makes contribution to the subject of homonymic conflict.[18] The next year he published a small volume, *La géographie linguistique*, which presents the entire subject in a manner adapted to the general reader. Numerous examples, taken, for the most part, from previous works, illustrate the principles he is discussing. His *Essais de géographie linguistique*, Deuxième Série, published in 1928, makes no explicit addition to the discussion of homonymic conflict, but the *Essais de géographie linguistique*, Nouvelle Série, 1938, includes several studies of particular significance.[19] Another student of the French vocabulary, Ernst

13. See, for instance, pp. 57–8, 29, 62.
14. Karl Jaberg, *Sprachgeographie. Beitrag zum Verständnis des Atlas linguistique de la France*, Aarau, 1908.
15. In *Archiv für das Studium der neueren Sprachen und Literaturen*, cxx (1908), 96–8.
16. In *Festschrift für Ernst Tappolet* (Basel, 1935), pp. 111–21.
17. *Société de Publications Romanes et Françaises*, xviii, 1936.
18. See, for example, the section "Le jars (oie mâle)," pp. 9–16.
19. A. Dauzat, *Essais de géographie linguistique*, Nouvelle Série, *Publications de la Société des Langues Romanes*, xxx, Montpelier, Paris, 1938.

Gamillscheg, has contributed a special treatise on the words for 'whet-stone' and 'trough' in France and adjacent regions,[20] several more recent studies,[21] and another general presentation of the subject of linguistic geography, *Die Sprachgeographie und ihre Ergebnisse für die allgemeine Sprachwissenschaft* (1928). In the latter he cites instances of the effects of homonymy not only from French, but also from works on the English, Scandinavian, Swiss vocabularies. He is circumspect, but clear, in his support of the theory of homonymic conflict.[22] Jacob Jud, writing in 1925, explains certain aspects of the history of words meaning 'éteindre' and 'déteindre,' as being the re-sult of conflict.[23]

Recognition of the significance of the theory has become ever more general, and with the work of Gilliéron and his immediate followers the theory of the conflict of homonyms may be said to have become the principle of the conflict of homonyms. It has continued to receive attention in a steadily increasing number of particular studies and in general works on language.[24]

It was not received, however, without criticism and objection. One such criticism, already referred to in these pages, was voiced in the *Festschrift* for Dr. Paul Kretschmer, published in 1926.[25] Elise Rich-ter, glancing over the subject of homonymy in many languages and discussing in particular the works of Gilliéron on the French vocabu-lary, takes objection to the theory at almost every point. Her objec-tions, to be made clear, would have to be given in detail, since she considers several particular instances—the study of *clavus-clavis*, of *molere-mulgere*, of *gallus-cattus*, etc.—and criticizes them at points

20. E. Gamillscheg, "Wetzstein und Kumpf im Galloromanischen," *Archivum Ro-manicum*, VI (1922), 1–104.

21. See the discussion of Gamillscheg's work in Iordan and Orr, *Introduction to Romance Linguistics*, pp. 235 ff.

22. *Archivum Romanicum*, VI, 10, note 1: "Es liegt mir ferne, der Homonymität unter allen Umständen zerstörende Wirkung zuzuschreiben. Aber es liegt auf der Hand, dass zwei Wörter, die in der gleichen Gesellschaftsschichte gleichzeitig eine wichtige Rolle spielen, die die gleichen syntaktischen Verbindungen eingehen können, und die beide Hauptwörter sind, auf die Dauer nicht lautlich zusammenfallen können, ohne in ihrer Verwendung diese Homonymität störend zu verspüren."

23. J. Jud, "Problèmes de géographie linguistique romane," *Revue de Linguistique Romane*, I (1925), 181–236. Jud's works, too numerous to be listed or discussed here, have played an important part in establishing the new scientific discipline of lin-guistic geography. See the discussion of them in Iordan and Orr, *Introduction to Ro-mance Linguistics*, pp. 226 ff.

24. Among recent works on the subject are studies of the French and Swiss vocabu-laries: the article by K. Jaberg, just mentioned, "Wie der Hundedachs zum Dachs und der Dachs zum Iltis wird"; L. Gauchat, "Interferenzen"; H. Kuen, "Beobachtungen an einem kranken Wort," all three published in the *Festschrift für Ernst Tappolet*, Basel, 1935. K. Jaberg's *Aspects géographiques du langage*, Paris, 1936, and I. Iordan and J. Orr's *Introduction to Romance Linguistics*, London, 1937, in which the develop-ment of the theory of homonymic confusion is sketched, have been mentioned.

25. Elise Richter. *Über Homonymie*, in *Festschrift für . . . Paul Kretschmer* (Vi-enna, Leipzig, New York, 1926), pp. 167–201.

differing from one to another. Her article is salutary rather than disconcerting for the proponent of the theory; it emphasizes the caution with which he must proceed. Not too easily and not without constant observation of all the possible circumstances involved, may he attribute the loss of particular words to homonymy. She touches upon one consideration that will perhaps play an increasingly important part as the theory of homonymic conflict is employed in future studies of language—that it is well to consider the history of the words concerned in all their manifestations, in Italian and Spanish as well as in French, for example. She cannot altogether refute the principle. Homonymic confusion remains a possible determining factor in a people's choice of synonyms and the disuse of some terms. But she believes that a language is more likely to avoid, in various ways, the formation of homonyms that may lead to confusion than to give up already existing words because of confusion between them. In the latter case, homonymy must be considered only a contributing factor, one of several causes leading to the disappearance of words.[26] Edwin B. Dike, to be mentioned again in connection with the theory in English, is sceptical of its soundness.[27] L. A. Terracher, in a brief sketch of the subject of linguistic geography, expresses a similar doubt, in a less emphatic way.[28] The theory has, however, gained general acceptance and holds a firm place in discussions of linguistic geography and of linguistic science in general.[29]

Interest in linguistic geography is by no means limited to France. The publication of the *Atlas linguistique de la France* gave great impetus to the study of dialects, not only among French scholars but elsewhere as well; it furnished materials so usable that scholars of many countries were immediately drawn into studying the dialects of "Galloromania." A very large body of new linguistic principles, or of principles developed and demonstrated in new ways, grew out of this interest, and thus France has seemed to lead the way, has actually

26. Richter, *Über Homonymie*, p. 200: "Mit diesen Gegenbemerkungen soll der bedeutende Anstoss, den Gilliéron durch die geographische Methode der Wortforschung gegeben, gewiss nicht verkleinert werden. Sicherlich ist es das natürliche Bestreben der Sprechenden, sich deutlich zu machen. Sprache ist in erster Linie Mittel der Mitteilung, und es unterliegt wohl keinem Zweifel, dass zahlreiche Wortgestaltungen, die sonst nicht zu begründen sind, auf das unbewusste Bestreben zurückgehen, Homonyme zu vermeiden. . . . Denn offenbar sind mehr Homonyme vermeiden, als schon vorhandene zerstört worden. Der hier unternommene Versuch . . . scheint zu dem Schluss zu berechtigen, dass nur ganz ausnahmsweise Homonymie allein der Grund sein kann, warum ein Wort ausser Gebrauch kommt."

27. See the following section.

28. L. A. Terracher, *Étude de géographie linguistique. Les Aires morphologiques dans les parlers populaires du nord-ouest de l'Angoumois (1800–1900)*, Bibliothèque de l'École des Hautes Études, Sciences historiques et philologiques, CCXII (1914), vi–vii.

29. See, for example, the discussion of linguistic geography, already referred to, in Iordan and Orr, *Introduction to Romance Linguistics*, Chap. 3.

led the way in many respects, in the development of this new branch of linguistic study. But some of the ideas on which it is based had developed contemporaneously in Germany. A linguistic atlas of Germany had been planned by Georg Wenker as early as 1876, and a small part of it published in 1881. Not until Wrede began publishing it again in 1926[30] was the large body of its material available for general use, but particular studies of the German dialects, based upon the *Atlas* and upon other investigations, have appeared at frequent intervals throughout the early years of the century and before.[31] By the time that Wenker's atlas was available, works on the French atlas had established the outlines of linguistic geography, in the sense in which that term is now used, and had spurred interest in similar kinds of investigation elsewhere.[32] The study of German dialects received this impetus and has advanced with great rapidity within the last twenty-five years. Much significant work has been done, notably that of Theodor Frings on the dialects of the Lower Rhine,[33] Kretschmer's investigation of High German from this point of view,[34] Pessler's general study of German linguistic geography.[35] Extremely important has been the series published under the direction of Wrede, *Deutsche Dialektgeographie,*[36] of which Frings' work referred to above constitutes one volume.

The principle of the conflict of homonyms is one part of linguistic geography and took form as a theory, or principle, in the works on the French vocabulary. But the ideas involved in it had also an apparently independent origin in Germany, though they did not reach full development. The works of Adelung, of Hirt, of Liebich have been cited in this connection.[37] Liebich, for example, writing in 1897,

---

30. *Deutscher Sprachatlas auf Grund des von Georg Wenker begründeten* SPRACH-ATLAS DES DEUTSCHEN REICHS, unter Leitung von Ferdinand Wrede, Marburg, 1926, and subsequent years.

31. A good discussion of the development of dialect study in Germany, with bibliographies, is to be found in Adolf Bach, *Deutsche Mundartforschung, Germanische Bibliothek,* XVIII, Heidelberg, 1934.

32. See data in J. Schrijnen, *Essai de bibliographie de géographie linguistique générale.*

33. Theodor Frings, *Studien zur Dialektgeographie des Niederrheins zwischen Düsseldorf und Aachen,* Marburg, 1910; published later as Vol. v of *Deutsche Dialektgeographie,* Marburg, 1913.

34. Paul Kretschmer, *Wortgeographie der hochdeutschen Umgangssprache,* Göttingen, 1918.

35. W. Pessler, *Deutsche Wortgeographie,* in *Wörter und Sachen,* XV (1933), 1–80.

36. F. Wrede, ed., *Deutsche Dialektgeographie, Berichte und Studien über G. Wenkers Sprachatlas des Deutschen Reichs,* Marburg, 1908, and subsequent years.

37. Miss Richter makes the same statement (*Über Homonymie,* p. 189): "Den massgebenden Leitsatz für die ganze Theorie vom Schwund infolge Homonymie hat Gilliéron ausgesprochen, der eigentliche moderne Vertreter, Ausgestalter und Verfechter der Homonymentheorie, wie denn die Romanisten überhaupt seit Diez sich öfter damit beschäftigt haben. . . ." In preceding pages she notes the early appearance of the idea in the works of Adelung (1782), of Jacobssohn, of Hirt, of Liebich.

within a few pages shadows forth the theory, in many of its aspects, as it was later developed in France.[38] He attributes the loss of particular words to their confusion with homonymous words; he maintains that, when conflict developed, one word might be supported both by frequency of use and by a wide "relationship" of words; he shows that in some cases only the homonym disappears, that derivatives, by virtue of their different form, might survive; he explains the presence of a dialectal form in the "Hochsprache" by the theory of homonymic confusion; he takes account of the fact that possible confusion may prevent the formation of new homonyms.[39] The explanation of actually existing homonyms is, for him, that the process of loss is an unfinished one, one complicated by many factors, varying in individual instances. His illustration from the history of the two verbs *lügen* and *liegen* is presented in a convincing manner; particularly notable is the fact that he supports his statements with historical data.[40] But, though several of the instances that he gives are striking, he failed to observe one thing that is fundamental to the principle as it developed later: he did not stress, or did not even see, that words must be used within the same realm of ideas if conflict is to be considered a factor in their history. It is scarcely probable that *enkel* 'ankle' and *enkel* 'grandchild,' that MHG *giht* 'confession' and *gicht* 'gout,' or even *hunt* 'hundred' and *hunt* 'dog' were mutually disturbing. More recent studies of German dialects also include the theory of homonymic conflict. Theodor Frings makes mention of it in his discussion of the relation of linguistic geography to broader philological knowledge.[41] He accepts the principle of conflict and adds to several examples cited from French studies an example from

38. B. Liebich, "Kleine Beiträge zur deutschen Wortforschung" (Breslau, 1897), in Paul and Braune, *Beiträge zur Geschichte der Deutschen Sprache und Literatur*, XXIII (1898), 223–31.

39. So an agent-noun in -er is formed for *malen,* not for *mahlen,* since a substitute for the latter was easily available.

40. In brief (and the illustration loses strength by the omission of his full explanation), he shows that MHG *ligen* 'jacēre' became NHG *līgen* by normal processes of vowel-lengthening, and that MHG *liegen* 'mentiri' became, by normal monophthongization, NHG *līgen*. There were thus two verbs *līgen*. Conflict ensued, as a result of which the present tense of *līgen* 'mentiri' died out and *lügen* took its place. The two forms *du leugst* and *er leugt,* which did not coincide in sound with corresponding forms of the homonym, survived longer and were still, in 1897, to be heard in the Silesian mountains.

It may, in this connection, be objected that the two words *lie* do exist in English. But examination indicates that there is little real possibility of confusion between them. Both are intransitive, both are common verbs, identical in forms of the present tense; but they are distinguished by syntactical constructions and context from the earliest times. "I think he is lying [speaking falsely]," but "I think he is lying down [reclining]." *Lie* 'recline' is normally accompanied by an adverbial modifier or prepositional phrase: "He is lying *on the bed, abed, on the grass, in wait, in ambush.*" *Lie* 'to speak falsely' is used independently.

41. Frings, *Sprachgeographie und Kulturgeographie,* pp. 550–3 in particular.

German.[42] His tone is humorous at times; but his reference to the principle of homonymy is serious. It holds, however, a minor place in his discussion; he believes that we should not stop with mere examples such as those that he offers, but should carry them always further and use them as additional means for understanding and explaining the cultural development of particular sections and countries, the "Sprachraume" that assume such importance in this discussion. Adolf Bach, in the work already referred to, mentions the possibility of loss of words through homonymy and gives as example Frings' instance of the conflict of *Fliege* and *Flöhe*.[43] An excellent study devoted entirely to the subject of homonymy in German was published by E. Öhmann in 1934.[44] After an introduction in which he sketches the appearance of the theory in the works of German scholars and others outside the field of Romance linguistics, he discusses the question of homonymic conflict in the German "Hochsprache" and dialects, giving examples of each of the effects it may have upon a language—word-loss, irregular sound-development established in certain accepted forms, "umbildungen, zusammensetzungen zur vermeidung der homonymie," etc. Among many instances, the study of the conflict of the verbs meaning 'blühen' and 'bluten' (pp. 27–33) is notable, showing as it does his careful consideration of the conflicting words and the "ersatzwort" in all their manifestations—in the standard vocabulary, in various dialects of Germany, and in languages other than German. He feels that the German language offers ample opportunity for investigation of homonymic conflict and its effects on language.[45]

There can be no attempt here to give a complete survey of discussions of homonymic conflict in Germany, such as that given in the introductory section of Öhmann's treatise. The above examples show that the principle has been found applicable to a study of the German vocabulary and German dialects. It is, however, less applicable to German than to either French or English. Modern High German is a more homogeneous language than English, has fewer borrowed words that have entered the language and shared its

42. Frings, *Sprachgeographie und Kulturgeographie*, p. 551: *Fliege* 'fly,' on a map showing the distribution of the word, does not appear in sections of central Germany, but is there replaced by South German *Mücke*. This observation must be connected, he says, with the fact that in those districts *Fliege* 'fly' and *Flöhe* 'flea,' in consequence of the loss of intervocalic -g- and unrounding, must have fallen together phonetically, "und die Flöhe die Fliege töteten wie im Gascognischen die Katze den Hahn."

43. Bach, *Deutsche Mundartforschung*, pp. 108–10.

44. E. Öhmann, *Über Homonymie und Homonyme im Deutschen*, in *Annales Academiæ Scientiarum Fennicæ*, Series B, 32.1 (1934), 1–143. He had published earlier, in 1931, a study of the preposition *after* in German, in which one of the most interesting aspects of homonymic conflict is considered, that is, the possible effects of conflict between words of obscene meaning and others; see *PBB*, LV (1931), 230–43.

45. *Op. cit.*, p. 3.

changes; it has experienced fewer marked phonological and morphological changes than have both French and English. There have been, therefore, fewer occasions for the coinciding, the "lautliche zusammenfall," of word-forms and consequently fewer instances of conflict. "Im Deutschen spielt, soweit man bis jetzt sieht (aber die Forschung hat das nachzuprüfen), der Wortschwund als Folge der Homonymie eine geringere Rolle als im Französischen."[46] The study of German dialects and the new atlases is, however, revealing an increasing number of instances of homonymic conflict, and lists such as Öhmann's of scholars who have turned their attention to the subject are indicative of the sustained interest with which it is being investigated.

As has been indicated in connection with the names of Jaberg and Jud, Switzerland has taken a place in the development of linguistic geography second only to that of France. Adolf Noreen has given examples of the conflict of homonyms in the Swedish language;[47] Caracostea and I. Iordan in Roumanian.[48] B. Trnka has written briefly on homonymy, with examples drawn from English and Czech.[49] L. A. Bulachovskij has written on conflict in the Slavic languages.[50] Linguistic atlases are appearing in ever-increasing numbers.[51] Most works of the kind have followed the initial studies of the data in the *Atlas linguistique de la France*. Gilliéron's work has proved dynamic in its power to stimulate further investigations.

46. Bach, *Deutsche Mundartforschung*, p. 110. See also Dauzat, *La géographie linguistique*, p. 71: "Dans les langues à évolution lente, comme l'italien, l'espagnol, l'allemand classique, où la prononciation se modifie insensiblement à travers les siècles, les homonymes sont rares et la fréquence des collisions se trouve excessivement réduite."

47. Adolf Noreen, "Ordens död," *Spridda Studier*, Andra Samlingen (Stockholm, 1903), pp. 126–37.

48. See reference to Caracostea in Schrijnen, *Essai de bibliographie de géographie linguistique générale*, p. 12, from which it is cited here. I. Iordan's *Introducere in Studiul Limbilor Romance* is the book that was augmented and revised by J. Orr, and published under the title *An Introduction to Romance Linguistics* (1937).

49. B. Trnka, "Bemerkungen zur Homonymie," *Travaux du Cercle Linguistique de Prague*, IV (1931), 152–6.

50. L. A. Bulachovskij, "De l'Homonymie dans les langues slaves," *Revue des Études Slaves*, VIII (1928), 68–80.

51. See the discussion in Iordan and Orr, *Introduction to Romance Linguistics*.

III

Works on Homonyms in English

SOME work has been done on the subject of homonymic conflict in English.[1] Between 1906 and 1912, four Kiel dissertations, dealing with the subject of loss of words in English, were published. Emil Hemken's was first, *Das Aussterben alter Substantiva im Verlaufe der englischen Sprachgeschichte*, published in 1906. Johannes Offe's on the loss of verbs and Wilhelm Oberdörffer's on adjectives followed in 1908, *Das Aussterben alter Verba und ihr Ersatz im Verlaufe der englischen Sprachgeschichte*, and *Das Aussterben altenglischer Adjektive und ihr Ersatz im Verlaufe der englischen Sprachgeschichte;* and four years later Friedrich Teichert's, a continuation and extension of the other three, appeared—*Über das Aussterben alter Wörter im Verlaufe der englischen Sprachgeschichte.*[2]

In all four works, homonymy and mutual conflict are assumed as one of the "inner or psycho-physical," that is, linguistic as opposed to social, causes of the loss of words. No one of the four pretends to a treatment of homonyms in any way exhaustive. Each gives lists of instances, stating, in a few sentences, two or more words that fell together in sound, and the substitute words for those that were lost. Oberdörffer's list of adjectives that have conflicted is very short; the others are long. In general the authors have observed the fundamental principles of the theory: their examples are usually words that were true homonyms at some point in their history and that were used within the same general circle of ideas. But this accuracy

1. Though it remained for recent investigators to develop the methods by which the effects of homonymic conflict can be discovered and demonstrated, interest in homonyms as such can be traced back to the earliest works on English grammar and language. In Christopher Cooper's *Grammatica Linguæ Anglicanæ*, London, 1685; in James Elphinston's *Principles of the English Language, Digested for the Use of Schools*, London, 1766; in John Murdoch's *Dictionary of Distinctions*, London, 1811, and others, appear long lists of homonyms variously arranged. They are given in an attempt, frequently, to demonstrate the "correct" pronunciation of words. Sometimes it is difficult to see just what purpose they could have served at the time they were published, though their potential value to linguists seeking to reconstruct English phonology is evident. Jespersen accompanies many of his discussions of sound-changes with lists of the homonyms that were produced by those changes: *A Modern English Grammar on Historical Principles*, 5th ed., London, 1933, and earlier editions.

2. Hemken is concerned for the most part with substantives from A through M, Offe and Oberdörffer take up verbs and adjectives through M and R respectively, each having based his work upon the *New English Dictionary*, at that time still incomplete; each adds words, however, from other sources. Teichert begins with words in M and takes up those through S, with additions. The four dissertations were written under the direction of Professor Ferdinand Holthausen, of Kiel, who reviewed them later.

fails at times. There is, for example, little probability of conflict between all the Old English words *ār—ār* 'honour,' *ār* 'oar,' *ār* 'ore,' *ār* 'messenger,' listed by Hemken.[3] The very multiplicity of terms with the same phonetic value may indeed have favored the adoption of synonyms for one or more of them, such as *honour*, when these became available, but it would be difficult to prove any real conflict between words used in such different connections as are *oar* and *honour*, *ore* and *oar*, *ore* and *messenger*. *Fihten* 'to fight' and *fihten* 'to moisten,' in Offe's group, would, almost certainly, be always distinguished by context, and by tone of voice in the case of oral expression.[4] *Gehyrstan* 'to murmur' and *hyrstan* 'to decorate' are hardly subject to confusion.[5] Teichert is, of the four, most careful to observe the determining circumstances of semantics, of use, and of chronology, and to add references to dialectal survivals. The importance of these inaccuracies is minimized by the larger number of instances cited in which phonetic identity and possibility of semantic confusion are not in question. The lists contain much material that can be used as basis for further investigation. But as real support for the theory of conflict they fall short, even in those respects in which the material available for the study offered particular advantages.[6] It was not to be expected that the authors could touch upon the dialectal distribution of the words in English; there was no place for such investigations in the plan of their works. But there should be, even in so brief a space, when conflict is presented as the cause of the disappearance of words, more proof given of the phonetic identity of the conflicting terms, more detailed account of the phonological processes involved. This question involves immediately another question, that of chronology. When did the various sound-changes bring particular words into conflict? Unless the investigator can show that loss or change was subsequent to the period at which the words became homonyms and could therefore have been confused, his evidence is of little real value to the general subject. The four writers have not, for reasons of economy, taken these points sufficiently into consideration. Their examples of homonymic conflict are rather a basis, often a firm basis, for further investigation by the student particularly interested in the subject than important contributions to the history of the theory.

Professor Holthausen's review of the four dissertations appeared in the *Germanisch-Romanische Monatsschrift* for the years 1915–19.[7] He sketches their subject matter, first giving a discussion of a similar

3. Hemken, *Das Aussterben alter Substantiva*, p. 30.
4. Offe, *Das Aussterben alter Verba*, p. 24.   5. *Ibid.*, p. 26.
6. These advantages and difficulties in the way of a study of the subject in English are discussed in the next section.
7. F. Holthausen, "Vom Aussterben der Wörter," *GRM*, vii (1915–19), 184–96.

work by Noreen on the Swedish vocabulary.[8] Brief mention is made of the sections, in each of the works, on the conflict of homonyms. He gives examples of words so lost, but adds nothing new to the subject.

In 1919, Sir Robert Bridges published, as a tract of the Society for Pure English, the work that he entitled *On English Homophones*. It has been a provocative article, for it is written in an exaggerated manner and many of his statements may easily be contradicted. He considers the frequency of homophones in English a defect of the language,[9] and as a preliminary step lists some 835 sets of homophones, arranged according to degree of possibility of their producing confusion. Then follows "a logical sequence" of separate statements that are, one by one, developed and illustrated.[10] The logic of the sequence would be perfect, perhaps, were each statement capable of proof. But the author maintains the exaggerated, very general, unscientific tone of his seven statements and almost succeeds in the end, very readable as most of his article is, in weakening by false claims the arguments for the theory of homonymy as a cause of the loss of words rather than supporting them. From the point of view of an English poet and stylist, homophones may conceivably be a "nuisance"; but proof of the statement that they constitute a troublesome defect in the language as a whole must be scientific and specific, and cannot be based upon generalizations.

After the completion of the *New English Dictionary*, a work similar in many respects to the four Kiel dissertations but superior to them was published, Kurt Jaeschke's *Beiträge zur Frage des Wortschwundes im Englischen*.[11] As those did, but in somewhat greater detail and with more careful attention to explanation of circumstances, he considers many causes of the loss of words, both social and purely linguistic; homonymy resulting in possible confusion is one of them. Not merely assuming it as a factor in the disappearance of words, he first states his belief in its soundness as a linguistic principle and explains the circumstances under which it operates.[12] His

8. See above, Chapter II, note 47.   9. Bridges, *On English Homophones*, p. 7.
10. *Ibid.*, p. 18:
  "1. Homophones are a nuisance.
  2. They are exceptionally frequent in English.
  3. They are self-destructive, and tend to become obsolete.
  4. This loss impoverishes the language.
  5. This impoverishment is now proceeding owing to the prevalence of the Southern English standard of speech.
  6. The mischief is being worsened and propagated by the phoneticians.
  7. The Southern English dialect has no claim to exclusive preference."
11. Breslau, 1931. He considers words from T to Z.
12. Jaeschke, *Beiträge*, p. 61: "Demnach ist wohl nicht mehr daran zu zweifeln, dass der Gleichklang als ein Faktor betrachtet werden muss, der den Wortschwund zur Folge haben kann."

observation that homonymy is more likely to lead to confusion between verbs than between substantives is an addition to discussions of the subject, though he dismisses it somewhat summarily. Then follows a series of instances of apparent conflict between words that resulted in loss of one or more. Each instance is briefly presented. More frequent mention is made of the time at which conflict occurred or disappearance was to be noted than in previous works, but in no instance is an example explained or analyzed in any great detail.

The point of view of the sceptic, as regards homonymic conflict, is to be found in Edwin B. Dike's "Obsolete Words," published in 1933.[13] This is a treatment of loss of words in English, briefer than Jaeschke's but filled with examples from the history of the English vocabulary. Homonymy as a destructive force he touches upon, as it were, in passing. He challenges the article by Bridges, showing that in Bridges' own prose are numerous homophones within a few lines. He concludes:

There is no way of knowing that homophony leads to obsolescence, and it is hard to capture a convincing pair of specimens. So dependent are we on written English that even where dates are close and all things favorable, we cannot be sure that confusion arising from sound-likenesses leads to disuse.[14]

Context in his opinion always saves the word from such confusion as might militate against its existence.

Gradually, however, the "pairs of specimens" have proved convincing, and the theory of conflict has gained acceptance. It is now usually accorded a place in histories of the language as one cause of loss of words. Leonard Bloomfield mentions it in *Language*[15] and offers examples. Weekley in *The Romance of Words* considers homonyms and even homonymic confusion, but from the point of view of attraction rather than of conflict, as do, also, Professors Greenough and Kittredge (*Words and Their Ways in English Speech*) and G. H. McKnight (*English Words and Their Background*).[16] In *The Psycho-Biology of Language*, Zipf assumes that confusion resulting from homonymy is a possible cause of the disappearance of words.[17]

There have been few independent works on homonymy in English.[18] B. Trnka, of Prague, published in 1931 his brief but significant

13. Edwin B. Dike, "Obsolete Words," *Philological Quarterly*, XII (1933), 207–19.
14. *Ibid.*, p. 215.   15. Bloomfield, *Language*, pp. 396–99 and elsewhere.
16. Ernest Weekley, *The Romance of Words*, London, 1912; Greenough and Kittredge, *Words and their Ways in English Speech*, New York, 1931; G. H. McKnight, *English Words and Their Background*, New York, 1931.
17. *Op. cit.*, pp. 30–3.
18. W. Schumann's *Die Homonyma der englischen Sprache*, Marburg, 1906, may be disregarded in this connection. It is a collection of puns, riddles, anecdotes, etc., illustrating the existence of homonyms in English.

article "Bemerkungen zur Homonymie."[19] It is primarily of a theoretical nature and touches on certain general principles involved in discussions of homonymy—the origin of homonyms; the relation of homonymy to monosyllabism, especially in English; the general question of the possibility of confusion between homonymous words; the possible relation of homonymy to the processes of sound-change in a language, a point that constitutes his most important contribution to discussions of the subject. His examples are for the most part drawn from English, with a few from French and from Czech.

A study of the verb *do* in English, "Syntaktische Homonymie: Das Umschreibende DO," by H. Marchand, appeared in 1938–39, which takes as one of its basic principles the effect of homonymic interference in the history of this verb.[20]

Erika Branys, in her *Homonyme Substantive im Neuenglischen,*[21] examines an extensive list of homophones in present-day English in an effort to determine the circumstances surrounding them—sociological, stylistic, semantic—in the midst of which they are tolerated in the language. Such investigation should, she feels, throw light on the question of word-loss because of homonymic confusion. She reiterates with added emphasis the importance, in all such studies, of considering words in relation to their context and in their syntactical relationships. Aside from this, her work adds little to the further development of the theory in English, but serves only to repeat, from another point of view and less clearly, Gilliéron's dictum that words concerned in homonymic conflict must be within the same sphere of thought and use: if they are not, then they are not subject to confusion and the cause of their loss must be sought elsewhere.

The most important single article on the conflict of homonyms in English is that by Professor Robert J. Menner, published in *Language,* in 1936.[22] Professor Menner considers the whole problem briefly, defining it and illustrating by various examples from the French and English vocabularies. The article is particularly valuable for its clear-cut presentation of the general status of the subject and for its suggestions as to methods of approach open to future investigators interested in this cause of the loss of words. He suggests, with convincing illustrations from the English vocabulary, that the "relation of homonymic interference to the borrowing of French words in English is worth considering"; that the striking changes that took place in Middle English in the inflection of verb and pronoun might be, in part, explained by application of this principle; and finally that "the

19. *Travaux du Cercle Linguistique de Prague,* IV, 152–6.
20. In *Englische Studien,* LXXIII (1938–39), 227–52.
21. Dissertation, Berlin, 1938.
22. Robert J. Menner, "The Conflict of Homonyms in English," *Language,* XII (1936), 229–44.

problem of homonymic conflict is connected with the problem of the limits of the word," that the "study of homonymic interference involves the whole problem of the word as an entity and illustrates some fundamental principles of semantics."

IV

Methods of Investigation

ANY detailed study of the theory of homonymic conflict in English must, of necessity, differ in method and in emphasis from corresponding studies in French or in German. The difference is that between the more strictly geographical approach and the historical, and is occasioned by the nature of the material available in the different countries for a study of the question. France and Germany have linguistic atlases. England has no linguistic atlas but does have the rich resources of the *New English Dictionary on Historical Principles* and numerous dialect dictionaries and glossaries, Joseph Wright's *English Dialect Dictionary*[1] being chief among them.

The lack of a dialect atlas in English is a serious initial difficulty in the way of a study of homonymic conflict. The whole subject grew, as has been shown, out of Gilliéron's investigation of material charted in the *Atlas linguistique de la France;*[2] the advantages offered by material of that nature are at once evident. To begin with, he and other investigators of the subject had before them the complete picture of the geographical distribution in France of a particular word or phrase.[3] They knew, with considerable accuracy, the dialectal form of a word or the dialectal equivalent of that word, at that particular time, in each of the localities given. Thus dividing lines between varying types, the different derivation-forms of a common original word, could be drawn with some degree of exactness. In the second place, they knew the sound of the words in each instance. Edmont recorded the responses to his 2,000 or more questions in phonetic notation, and succeeding investigations have revealed the very high degree of accuracy which he attained in this respect. Later interpreters did not have to build up, by reference to known phonological processes, by comparison of variant spellings of words, and by study of occasional

1. Joseph Wright, ed., *The English Dialect Dictionary*, London, New York, 1898–1905.

2. A description of the plan of the *Atlas linguistique* and the methods by which the material in it was collected and compiled by Edmont and Gilliéron, under the direction of the latter, has been given too frequently for a repetition to be necessary here. For such accounts see Dauzat, *La géographie linguistique*, Chap. 1; Gamillscheg, *Die Sprachgeographie*, pp. 1–5; and Gilliéron's own statements of his plans in *Atlas linguistique de la France*. NOTICE *servant à l'intelligence des cartes*, Paris, 1902. For a brief comparison of the advantages and disadvantages for dialect study of this kind of atlas and the German atlas, compiled by quite different methods, see E. C. Roedder, "Linguistic Geography," *Germanic Review*, 1 (1926), 300 ff.

3. Not all the charts, or maps, give the distribution throughout France. Some are half, some are quarter maps, giving the appearance of word or phrase in certain sections only.

records of pronunciation, the phonetic value of particular forms in particular areas. That material was at their command from the beginning and could be presented graphically and accurately on maps that did much to clarify their discussions.[4] French students deal then, so to speak, with completed processes. That factor that kept *gat (from gallus) from developing in Gascony, or caused its disappearance when it did develop, has already operated. The maps show clearly, in this and similar instances, the absence of the word at the present time, and investigators can safely "build backward" from the known phenomena of the present to the probable reasons for them in the past.

The clarity of outline and the fullness of material thus made possible in their studies tend to conceal one point of weakness, do indeed keep it from being a significant weakness. Their materials do not furnish the longitudinal pictures, so to speak, of the terms concerned, the chronology of the linguistic processes under consideration. When did *gat (from gallus) coincide in sound with gat (from cattus), when, that is, did the process by which final -ll developed into -t in Gascony operate? Is there evidence historically that the words did exist in that area before homonymy developed and that disappearance followed homonymy? The French authors reach such conclusions generally by methods other than historical ones: occasional appearances of a form in areas of disappearance, and the relative contours of adjacent areas where the word persists, for example, lead them to believe that originally the word did exist throughout the whole area. Their reasoning is generally satisfactory, but one could wish now and then for more of the historical view,[5] more accurate account of the chronology of the processes they discuss.

Almost directly opposed to these advantages and difficulties are those offered by available sources of material in English. There is no dialect atlas of England. The dialectal forms and pronunciation of a word must be sought in Wright's *English Dialect Dictionary*, in glossaries of varying degrees of completeness, and in a few dictionaries of the dialects of particular localities that have more recently been compiled and that take more carefully into account the importance of accurate phonetic transcription of sounds heard in those dialects.[6] These are unsatisfactory to one seeking a fairly com-

4. It is, of course, true that certain limitations are necessarily attendant upon the methods of Gilliéron and Edmont and that their material should, ideally, be supplemented by other kinds. The limitations are discussed by Dauzat, *La géographie linguistique*, pp. 9 ff. But much can safely be based upon their data alone.

5. The historical background of homonymic conflicts, though usually disregarded by Gilliéron himself, is considered in the work of such followers as Jud and Jaberg.

6. Cf., for example, W. E. Haigh, *A New Glossary of the Dialect of the Huddersfield District*, London, 1928; Sir Alfred Pease, *A Dictionary of the Dialect of the North Riding of Yorkshire*, Whitby, 1928.

plete picture of the distribution of a word or words at a given time. Wright, for example, gives pronunciations heard in dialect and then lists the counties where they are heard, with illustrations of the use of the term. But he does not specify which pronunciation is peculiar to a given county or section. We must determine that, usually, by study of the spelling, too often an unreliable basis for conclusions as to phonetic values, and by reference, when possible, to more specific dialect dictionaries and studies such as that of Kökeritz of the Suffolk dialect and W. Grant's of the English of Scotland,[7] that treat the phonology of the dialect but give little evidence of vocabulary. Then, too, the scattered nature of this material makes it impossible to construct a picture that is altogether reliable from point of view of time. Wright's *English Dialect Dictionary* was published from 1898 to 1905; Jamieson's *Etymological Dictionary of the Scottish Language* from 1879 to 1882;[8] Haigh's *Dialect of the Huddersfield District* in 1928; Pease's *Dictionary of the Dialect of the North Riding of Yorkshire* in 1928. There is thus a discrepancy in time, in material collected from all these sources, that is often negligible but may, in some cases, be significant. Again, Wright's *English Dialect Dictionary*, our most important source of information on the dialects of England, gives occurrence of terms by counties. Thus maps that may be constructed on his data, such as the one accompanying the study of *gate* in the following pages, must be approximate as to geographical lines, cannot have the exactness that Gilliéron's material, collected from 639 communities, affords.

As a result, the student of the subject in English must approach it by ways different from those followed so successfully by the French philologists. He cannot expect to demonstrate the potential destructive force of homonymy on the vocabulary with the mathematical exactness that they can command in their maps and analyses. His conclusions as to dialectal distribution, at a given time, must be tentative, based as they are upon incomplete data, until much more extensive investigation has been made of the dialects of England. He must, indeed, adopt a different means of approach to his subject.

The material of the *New English Dictionary on Historical Principles* makes a different approach possible. He may, indeed must, adopt the historical point of view. The English language, like the French, is peculiarly suited to a study of the conflict of homonyms. It has

7. Helge Kökeritz, *The Phonology of the Suffolk Dialect, Descriptive and Historical,* Uppsala, 1932; W. Grant, *The Pronunciation of English in Scotland,* Cambridge, 1913; W. Grant and J. M. Dixon, *Manual of Modern Scots,* Cambridge, 1921; W. Grant, *The Scottish National Dictionary,* Edinburgh, 1931, and subsequent years.

8. John Jamieson, *An Etymological Dictionary of the Scottish Language,* new edition by J. Longmuir and D. Donaldson, Paisley, 1879–82. *Supplement,* Paisley and London, 1887.

undergone many sound-changes by which sounds, originally distinct, coincided; OE *e*, OE *ǣ*, OE *ēa*, for example, under particular circumstances, all became ME *ę̄*. Many homonyms were created in this way at successive periods. And it has been enriched by stores of words taken over, in consequence of the vicissitudes of history, from neighboring languages, words that, subjected to the sound-laws of the English language, not infrequently became homonymous with other borrowed words or with native terms already existing in the language. The dictionary, by giving the earliest recorded instances of the use of a term in English, by giving the last recorded use of words now obsolete, by tracing chronologically the changes in form and the shifting in sense of each word, and by its frequent reference to the "habitat" of uncommon words and its quotations from documents of the Middle English period that may often be located, accurately or approximately, has made available abundant material for a study of homonymic conflict. The student, possessed of knowledge of the phonological processes affecting the language, can trace this development chronologically. If words, incompatible in meaning according to the principles outlined in preceding pages, become homonyms at a given time; if the dictionary shows that one or both becomes obsolete or archaic in Standard English within a given time subsequent to this period; if substitute terms begin to appear with greater frequency at the time that homonymy may be supposed to have developed; if dialect dictionaries give evidence that the words survive in dialects where homonymy did not develop—then the student may draw the conclusion that homonymy was an active factor in their history. Questions of chronology thus become of paramount importance.

It may be, perhaps, even fortunate for the study of homonyms that the records in English are historical in their emphasis rather than geographical. For the English vocabulary includes an unusual number of borrowed terms, and the time of the appearance in English of words borrowed from Scandinavian, or French, for example, may, in a study of homonymic conflict, be significant. Their entrance may have been facilitated, or their position in the language established, by the need, at that particular time, of substitute terms for words weakened by collision with other words; or, if we follow literally the theory of Teichert, homonymy may be said to have been the determining element in the choice of synonyms, all existing in the language but some more favorably situated than others. The student of the subject in English must, then, base his conclusions upon facts of chronology supported and amplified by observations, necessarily incomplete, as to geographical distribution.

V

Plan and Purpose of the Present Work

IT is from such materials that the following studies have been developed. They are attempts to demonstrate the soundness of the theory of conflict as an alleged cause of the loss of words from the English vocabulary. The list is in no sense exhaustive; but the study of each instance is as exhaustive as materials would permit. All sources of information conceivably connected with the history of the words have been sought. Thus the works on English place-names were consulted in the attempt to determine the geographical distribution of the words *gate;* Jamieson's *Scottish Dictionary* and Wright's *English Dialect Dictionary,* with all available special studies of dialects, have been constantly referred to. The data in the *New English Dictionary* form the basis of the whole.

It has been found expedient to group together certain instances that illustrate a given sound-change or related series of changes; OE æȝ, OE ǣȝ, OE eȝ, OF *ai,* etc., for example, all became ME *ai,* causing the coinciding of several words originally distinct, and instances of homonyms so created have been considered together. Several instances called for individual and separate treatment.

There has been no attempt to establish a logical order in discussing the various examples, such as Professor Menner suggests in his article. Each instance, or group of instances, has been analyzed and investigated as a separate study, and the attempt has been made to show that in particular cases and under given circumstances the confusion arising from homonymy of words may indeed serve to weaken the position of one or more of them and eventually to cause their disappearance. As the number of such demonstrations increases, lines of classification will presumably develop and homonyms may be studied in groups as illustrations, for example, of the rôle played in English by French or by Scandinavian, as illustrations of the causes of change in the English pronoun or verb systems. The purpose of the present work is to demonstrate the soundness of the theory of homonymic conflict as a cause of loss of words from the English language and to show the abundant sources of material for a study of the English vocabulary along lines made clear by the recent work in linguistic geography.

The instances considered involve words that are, throughout their history in English, different words, derived from different languages or from different periods of one language. In most cases words in each group may be traced to different ultimate sources. This does not imply, however (and the point justifies a digression), that the principle involved in homonymic conflict is limited to this category. Conflicting terms may be different words, etymologically, or the same word in different senses; the principle is the same. Gilliéron has developed this idea in connection with the French vocabulary;[1] Jespersen assumes it in his work on monosyllabism in English; Menner discusses its theoretical significance in his article on the conflict of homonyms in English.[2] If a single word develops mutually antagonistic senses, senses that are not distinguished by modifying or limiting constructions, then in one or both it is likely to lose its status and be replaced by substitutes. Thus the principle involved may prove to be the cause of enrichment of the vocabulary. New words must be borrowed, or unambiguous variant formations of the same word must be invented to take the place of those that have become unsuitable for use. Gilliéron gives, among other examples, that of *sanctify* and *sanction:* "Le xviie s. allait nous donner le droit de dire qu'un mot est SANCTIFIÉ par l'usage. Nous avons raison, ce nous semble, de le remplacer par SANCTIONNÉ."[3] Exactly the same phenomenon is to be observed in English, at about the same time. The history of the English words *convent* and *convention* indicates, in the same way, that genuine conflict may occur between different senses of the same word.

Convent meant from early times both 'an institution founded for the living together of a number of "religious" persons, monks, friars, nuns, etc.' and the less specific 'an assemblage or gathering of persons.' But as the specific sense became more and more fixed, and was extended to mean even the buildings occupied by such a religious community,[4] the more general meaning was taken over by *convention.*

<hr>

1. Gilliéron, *L'Abeille,* pp. 258–9: "Car, en dehors de l'enrichissement apporté par des termes nouveaux correspondant à des objets nouveaux, à des idées nouvelles, il y a à la base de la création des mots dits savants ou semi-savants des raisons d'être dans l'inaptitude des mots auxquels il se sont substitués ou à côté desquels ils sont venus se ranger.

"Cette substitution et cette coexistence ont leur origine dans le besoin de clarté, dans le besoin de distinguer les uns des autres des homonymes de sémantique différente et des sémantiques différentes dans un seul et même mot, d'effacer dans la langue deux éléments d'obscurité, la sursaturation phonétique et la sursaturation sémantique, qui, en réalité, ne sont qu'un seul état pathologique, réclamant la même médication, la substitution.

"L'état pathologique a été engendré d'une part par la convergence en un même point de l'action de lois mécaniques (collision formelle des mots), d'autre part par la convergence en un même point de perceptions et de conceptions psychologiques (collision sémantique dans un mot).

". . . on voit tous les jours la langue littéraire créer des néologismes pour ne pas employer des mots existants, de crainte que leur emploi ne crée un bissémantisme qu'il importe de fuir, parce que . . . la place est occupée. . . ."

2. *Language,* XII, 243–4.   3. Gilliéron, *L'Abeille,* p. 259.
4. *NED,* see *Convent.* 5.

Convent in the sense 'assemblage or gathering' is obsolete after the middle of the seventeenth century; *convention,* first introduced from French or directly from Latin about 1490, began to be used to mean 'an assembly or gathering of persons for some common object' about the middle of the sixteenth century and has now superseded *convent* entirely in this sense.

Though this is a significant and interesting aspect of the whole subject, discussions have been here limited to conflict between words, different etymologically, that have, by normal phonological development, become homonyms.

The phonetic system adopted for this work is the simplified (or "broad") form of the International Phonetic Alphabet as it is used by Daniel Jones in his *An English Pronouncing Dictionary* (London and Toronto, New York, 1917), and *The Pronunciation of English* (Cambridge, 1924). This is used throughout for Modern English sounds, except in a few cases where another system has, for particular reasons, been followed; in such cases, definite note is made of the fact. For Middle English sounds, the system usual in such grammars of the period as Jordan's *Handbuch der mittelenglischen Grammatik*[5] and Luick's *Historische Grammatik der englischen Sprache*[6] has been used, with frequent transliteration into corresponding symbols of the IPA.

5. Richard Jordan, *Handbuch der mittelenglischen Grammatik,* in *Germanische Bibliothek,* Samml. 1, Reihe 1, Band 13, Heidelberg, 1925.
6. Karl Luick, *Historische Grammatik der englischen Sprache,* Leipzig, 1921.

STUDIES

I

Conflict of Ear *and* Near

"Let other poets raise a fracas
'Bout vines, an' wines, an' drucken Bacchus,
An' crabbit names an' stories wrack us,
⠀⠀⠀⠀An' grate our lug:
I sing the juice Scotch bear can mak us,
⠀⠀⠀⠀In glass or jug."

So Burns writes in his lively poem, *Scotch Drink*.[1]

" 'Ah! . . . these are changed days since your cousin and I heard the balls whistle in our lugs,' " Stevenson has one of his characters say to another in *Catriona*.[2]

"What fahin lugs t' dog's gitten," says the countryman of the North or East Riding of Yorkshire.[3]

"Ye canna make a silk purse o' a sow's lug," runs one of David Fergusson's Scottish proverbs.[4]

What has happened to the word *ear* in northern England and Scotland, where such expressions as these are commonly to be heard in colloquial and dialectal speech? For *lug* means 'ear' in those sections of Britain; it is, indeed, according to numerous authorities, the only word for 'ear' in certain areas. The *NED* says that *lug* "in colloquial Sc. use has entirely superseded the older word [i.e., *ear*]," that it is "In Sc. the only word in use, *ear* being obs. exc. in combination."[5] Jamieson says that *lug* is "the common term for this member of the body [the ear] in S. as well as A. Bor."[6] Numerous glossaries of dialects indicate the same thing. Why has *ear* been to a great extent thus replaced by *lug?* The reasons are to be found in the history of these two words, in their relation to a third.

The word *ear* has a long and clear history among English substantives. It can be traced back directly to early Old English times and, through a study of its cognates in West and North Germanic and

1. Robert Burns, *Scotch Drink*, in *Complete Poetical Works of Robert Burns* (Cambridge Edition, Boston, 1897), pp. 4 ff. See also *NED*, under *Lug*.
2. R. L. Stevenson, *Catriona* (London, Paris, and Melbourne, 1893), p. 52. See also *NED*, under *Lug*.
3. M. C. F. Morris, *Yorkshire Folk-Talk* (London and York, 1892), p. 339.
4. Reference in Jamieson, *Etymological Dictionary of the Scottish Language*, under *Lug*, sb., to "Fergusson's S. Prov.," p. 35."
5. *NED*, under *Lug*, sb.²
6. Jamieson, *Etymological Dictionary of the Scottish Language*, under *Lug*, sb. (S., abbr. for *Scotland;* A. Bor., *Anglia Borealis*).

Gothic, beyond Old English to its hypothetical source-word in Germanic:

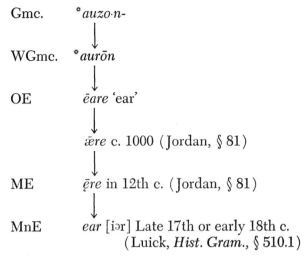

Gmc.   *auzo·n-

WGmc.   *aurōn

OE   ēare 'ear'

          ǣre c. 1000 (Jordan, § 81)

ME   ẹ̄re in 12th c. (Jordan, § 81)

MnE   ear [iər] Late 17th or early 18th c.
          (Luick, *Hist. Gram.*, § 510.1)

Even so early as in Old English times numerous compounds and derivatives were formed from it: OE *ēarliprica* 'flap of the ear,' *ēarhring* 'ear-ring,' *ēarplættan* 'to strike on the ear,' *ēarwærc* 'ear-ache,' *ēargespreca* 'whisperer,' *ēarwicga* 'earwig,' etc. It has been firmly established in the language from the beginning.

But in the early part of the 16th century there appeared the synonym *lug*, which, as has been indicated, has almost supplanted the older substantive in Scotland and part of England. It was used by 16th- and 17th-century English writers as "a slang or jocular synonym" for *ear;* Ben Jonson in *A Staple of News*,[7] for example, has the humorous character Peni-boy Canter say in a rage, " 'A fine round head, when those two lugs are off, To trundle through a Pillory.' " And when Shirley brings the quarrel of the two pages in *The Contention of Ajax and Ulysses*[8] to its height, one of them shouts, " 'Sirrah, 'tis I pronounce, [that] if you have A mind to lose one of your lugs, or quit Some teeth . . . Or run the hazard of an eye . . . Talk on, and when it is too late, you may Repent your impudence.' " In the early Scottish records, on the other hand, the word seems to have an entirely serious connotation, being used in various official records of punishments, etc. Its etymology and origin are obscure. The *NED* offers only a suggestion in regard to either:

7. Ben Jonson, *The Staple of News* 5.2.89–90 (*Yale Studies in English*, xxviii [1905]). See also *NED* and Jamieson, *Etymological Dictionary of the Scottish Language*, under *Lug*.

8. James Shirley, *The Contention of Ajax and Ulysses for the Armour of Achilles*, Sc. i, in *The Dramatic Works and Poems of James Shirley* (London, 1833), vi, 374. See also *NED*, under *Lug*.

Presumably this application [i.e., as a synonym for *ear*] is a transferred use of a word that existed earlier with some other meaning. It is possible that the sense 'earflap of a cap,' which is the earliest represented in our quots., may really be prior to the sense 'ear'; for similar transferences of words from parts of clothing to the parts of the body covered, cf. *breech, crown, sole.* If so, the word may perh. be of Scandinavian origin, with a general sense of 'something that can be pulled or laid hold of,' specialized differently in Sw. *lugg* forelock, with which cf. Eng. dial. (Sheffield, North Derb., etc.) 'to pull (somebody's) lugs,' meaning not as in Scotland, the ears, but the hair.

The same uncertainty is to be noted in Scandinavian dictionaries that list this word.[9] Its origin is obscure, but its presence in English dialect is clearly and fully recorded. It is found in Cornwall, in the sense 'ear,' but is predominantly, in that sense, a Northern word, appearing in all of England north of a line drawn from west to east along the southern borders of Cheshire, Derbyshire, Nottinghamshire, Lincolnshire, Norfolk, Suffolk (see map for this study, p. 55). South of that large area, the word *lug* appears, but in a different sense, with no apparent connection with *lug* 'ear.' It means there 'a pole, a long stick, a measure of length, etc.' (Cf. *Lug*, sb.[1] in *NED.*)

Conflict between two words, capable of confusion in use because both are names for parts of the body, and phonetically identical in certain much-used sentence-constructions (in some districts identical as independent words), has helped to establish the word *lug* 'ear' in Scotland and the North of England. *Lug* replaces *ear* in those areas because *ear* has there come into conflict with *near, ear* 'kidney.'

In Middle English about the beginning of the 14th century, there first appears in documents the word *nēre* meaning 'kidney.' Its history is, in the absence of records, not definitely known. It probably represents an OE *nēora or *nēore, corresponding to OHG *nioro, niero*, and ON *nȳra*.[10] In that case the ME form was *nēre*, with the close *ē* + *r* that became [iər] in the 16th century (Luick, *Hist. Gram.*, §§ 480, 505). From the 14th to the 17th centuries it was apparently a common word, records of its appearance being relatively numerous; but it was, perhaps, even then more usual in the North and Midlands than in the South, Scotland, Nottinghamshire, Norfolk being represented in four of the first six quotations given for it in the *NED.*[11] From the 14th century it shared its function with the word *kidney* (first recorded in *NED* c.1325). *Kidney* is also a word of obscure history. It appears in the forms *kidenei* (sing.) *kid(e)neris, kyd-*

9. See *Lugg* in H. S. Falk and Alf Torp, *Norwegisch-Dänisches etymologisches Wörterbuch, Germanische Bibliothek,* Samml. 1, Reihe 4, Bd. 1, Heidelberg, 1910–11.
10. See *NED*, under *Neer.*
11. 1300 *E. E. Psalter* (Notts.); c1375 *Sc. Leg. Saints* (Scotl.); 1440 *Promp. Parv.* (Norf.); 1549 *Compl. Scot.*

neers (pl.), etc. According to both the *NED* and Wyld[12] the origin of the first element, *kid-*, is unknown; the second element is given by both as probably from ME *ey*, pl. *eyren*, etc. 'egg,' the *NED* adding that the "pl. *kid(e)neris* might possibly owe its form to association with *neres, neeres*, pl. of *nere* [meaning 'kidney']." Though interesting, its exact origin is not consequential to the present study. Of greater moment is the fact that this word had, by the beginning of the 18th century, taken over in Standard English the function of both words (i.e., *kidney* and *near* 'kidney'), and *nere, neer* 'kidney' was restricted to dialect.

It was not to be expected that both *ear* 'ear' and *neer, nere* 'kidney' should remain in Standard English. During Middle English times the two were quite distinct phonetically as well as semantically, as has been pointed out. *Ear* had open $\bar{e} + r$, from OE $\bar{e}a + r$; *nere* had close $\bar{e} + r$, from OE $\bar{e}o + r$. But when $\bar{e}$ə [ɛːə] from ME $\bar{e}$ before *r*, with the [ə]-sound which had developed between $\bar{e}$ and *r*, $\bar{e}$ and *r*, etc. at the end of the 15th century (Luick, *Hist. Gram.*, § 505), became first $\bar{e}$ə [eːə] and then [iə] about the middle of the 17th century (Luick, *Hist. Gram.*, § 510.1), $\bar{e}re$ 'ear' thus becoming [iər], the two words were no longer distinct in sound. For *nēre* had reached the same vowel-grade in the course of the 16th century: $\bar{e} + r$ became [iər] (Luick, *Hist. Gram.*, § 480, § 505).

Ear 'ear' and *nere* 'kidney' were, therefore, in Standard English [iər] and [niər] respectively. The initial *n-* of the latter did not serve to differentiate them. When used with the indefinite article or with certain of the possessive pronouns the two words become identical; *an ear, a near; min ear, my near*, particularly in quick colloquial speech, are not to be distinguished.[13] Instances of actual and permanent transference of the *-n* of the article to the following substantive and of loss of initial *n-* of the substantive are well-known: *adder* from OE *næddre; apron* from OF *naperon; nickname* from earlier *an ekename*. The opening quotation under *neer* in the *NED* shows the word in use in just such circumstances: "*a* 1300 E. E. Psalter lxxii. 21 Mi neres ere torned for unquert." It was inevitable that confusion should arise among speakers when words denoting different parts of the body, words that are frequently in demand in common parlance, thus became homonymous. *Ear* remained in the standard language. *Nere, near* 'kidney' is not recorded, except in dialect, after the 16th century; there is a gap in records for it during the 17th century, the time when confusion with *ear* was likely, and by the 18th century it appears as a strictly dialectal word, *kidney* taking its place in Standard English.

12. Wyld, *The Universal Dictionary of the English Language*, London, 1932.

13. *Min, myn(e, mine*, poss. pron., were commonly used before vowels and *h*, in southern and Midland England, until the 18th century. See *NED*, under *Mine*, poss. pron.

In dialects, also, *ear* and *nere, near* are mutually exclusive. *Near* 'kidney,' always more common in the North than in the South, has remained in the dialects and colloquial speech of Scotland and of the Northern and North Midland counties of England. (See map, p. 55.) It was probably supported in those sections by the influence of the cognate word in Old Norse, *nȳra* 'kidney.' Suffolk *nire, nyre* forms indicate a direct relation to this word (cf. *NED*). And in almost exactly the same area in which *near, ear* is used to mean 'kidney,' as reference to the map will show, *lug* has taken the place of the *ear* 'ear' which we should expect to find there.

The same possibility of confusion between *ear* and *near* exists here as in Standard English, perhaps to an even greater degree than in Standard English, for country people, especially farming people, would have more frequent occasion, it is likely, to use the term for kidney—in connection with animals, as an article of diet, etc.—than would the people of London, for example. That the *n-* of *near* does not preclude confusion is more or less proved by the existence, in Scotland, Northumberland, Durham, and Suffolk, of a form without *n-*: *ears*, says Jamieson, means 'kidneys' in Dumfries and Lothian; *ear*, sb.[3] in the *English Dialect Dictionary*, means 'kidney' in Scotland, Northumberland, Durham, Cumberland, and Suffolk; W. Dickinson lists *ear* 'kidney' and *ear fat* 'the fat surrounding the kidney' as in general use in Cumberland.[14]

And the vowel-sounds from OE *ēa* + *r* and *ēo* + *r* coalesced generally in these northern sections, as in the standard language. Evidence presented in Wright's *English Dialect Grammar* is conclusive on this point. It is given, with explanation, in chart form in the note appended to this study. Both OE *ēa* + *r* and OE *ēo* + *r* became MnE [iə(r][15] in most of the area under discussion. This is very clearly evident in Scotland, Cumberland, Westmorland, Northumberland, Durham, Yorkshire, Lancashire, Lincolnshire, Derbyshire (see chart, p. 54). In northeast Norfolk *ēa* in *ear* 'ear' took the sound [ɑ:]; but in south Norfolk the two sounds coalesce, not as [iə], but as [ɛə]; thus *an ear* and *a near*, if both appeared in south Norfolk, would have been homonymous there, as they were in other parts of Scotland and England under a different sound, that is, [iə(r].

As has been stated elsewhere, maps of dialectal words in English must necessarily be approximate. Records of words are given, in such works as Wright's *English Dialect Dictionary*, by counties; occasionally we have detailed studies of particular sections such as that of Haigh on the dialect of Huddersfield. But in the case of *ear* 'ear' and *near* 'kidney,' all records demonstrate in a striking way the in-

14. W. Dickinson, *A Glossary of the Words and Phrases Pertaining to the Dialect of Cumberland*, re-arranged by E. W. Prevost, London, Carlisle, 1899.

15. Wright's phonetic notation has been changed here and in the chart into the corresponding IPA symbols.

fluence that homonymy may exert upon the distribution of words. The map, based chiefly on Wright's and Jamieson's records, shows (to repeat) that in almost exactly the same area in which the dialectal representative of ME *nere* appears for 'kidney,' *lug* is used for 'ear.' *Ear* 'organ of hearing' and *near, nere, ear* 'kidney' became, under certain rather common circumstances, homonyms, and conflict necessarily followed; *near* remained in use, *ear* was replaced by *lug*.

Lug 'ear' is found in four counties where *near* 'kidney' is not recorded. In one of these, a corrupted form of *near* (*nurses* 'kidneys' in northeast Lancashire, now obsolete) indicates that *near* has not been entirely unknown there. All these counties, with the exception of Cornwall, are contiguous to the area where *near* meaning 'kidney' is used. On the other hand, *near* 'kidney' appears in one section, Warwickshire, where *lug* 'ear' is not recorded. Warwickshire is within an area where *lug* in a different sense is a commonly used dialect word (see map). More detailed phonological studies of the dialect of Warwickshire will in time reveal how the two terms *ear* and *near* are used in this section where, so far as present records show, they exist together.

Though they add nothing further to the general conclusions of this study, investigations of the dialect of certain specific districts reveal in an interesting way that the general observation is true in particular cases.

In the dialect of Huddersfield[16] all three words appear: *lug* here means 'the hair about the ears'; *nier* [niər] means 'a kidney'; and *yer* [jəːr] means 'an ear.' The last two are, in this case, not homophones.

The list of related words in Jamieson's *Scottish Dictionary* is an indication of the firm position of *lug* in Scottish. He gives *lug* 'the ear,' 'projecting handle of a vessel'; to *lug* 'to cut off one's ears' (Aberd.); *luggie* 'a game in which one is led around a circle by the ear'; *luggit* 'a cuff on the ear' (Shetl.); *lug-knot* 'a knot of ribbons attached to the ear or front of a female's dress'; *lug-lachet* 'a box on the ear' (Aberd.); *lug-mark* 'a mark cut in the ear of a sheep, that it may be known' (common Scottish); to *lug-mark* 'to make a slit or notch in the ear of a sheep'; 'to punish by cropping the ears.' *Neirs, neres* 'the kidneys' (common Scottish) and *ears* (in the *Supplement* also *eirs, eers*) 'kidneys' have been mentioned earlier in this study. *Ear* 'organ of hearing' is not given, unless *-ear* in *sky-ear* 'a projecting part of a plough' represents it.

In Dickinson's detailed work on the dialect of Cumberland, *ear* is recorded as being in general use for 'kidney,' *near* means 'kidney' in the southwest and northwest parts of the shire, *ear fat* 'the fat surrounding the kidneys' is general. *Lug* is the general term for the ear,

16. W. E. Haigh, *A New Glossary of the Dialect of the Huddersfield District.*

lug mark for ear-marks on sheep. *Ear* 'organ of hearing' appears only in the compound term, *ear-bit,* an east central term.[17]

In J. C. Atkinson's *Glossary of the Cleveland Dialect* appear *inear* 'the kidney,' *lug* 'the ear,' *lug-ends* 'the tips of the ears,' *near* 'a kidney.' *Ear* 'ear' is not given.

Similar lists might be made from Pease's *Dictionary of the Dialect of the North Riding of Yorkshire,* from W. Rye's *Glossary of Words Used in East Anglia,*[18] from Robinson's *Glossary of Words Used in the Neighbourhood of Whitby,* and others.

Such evidence is positive; of a less conclusive but very interesting nature is the indirect evidence implied in the history of the words *ear* 'ear' and *near* 'kidney' in other West Germanic languages, for example Dutch and High German, given here in diagram form:

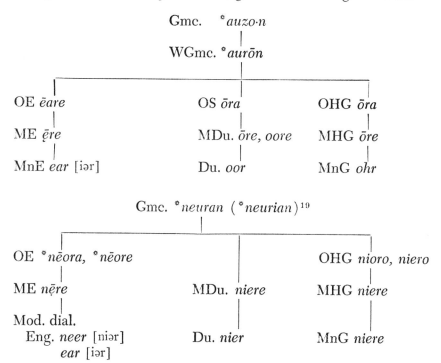

Only in English do the two terms develop phonetic similarity—by means of the indefinite article, homonymy. Only in English does the second term lose its place in the standard language and become a purely dialectal word.

17. W. Dickinson, *Glossary of the Words and Phrases Pertaining to the Dialect of Cumberland.*

18. Walter Rye, *A Glossary of Words Used in East Anglia,* English Dialect Society, Series C, Original Glossaries, No. 75, London, 1895.

19. Reconstructed forms taken from Falk-Torp. See *Nure*

Note on Phonology of OE *ēar* and *ēor* in Scotland and Midland and Northern Counties of England

The chart is based on the data in § 187 and § 195 and in the Index of Wright's *English Dialect Grammar*, 1905. Wright's phonetic symbols have been changed into those of the IPA.

The sounds that OE *ēar* in *ēare* 'ear' has taken are given. *Near* 'kidney' is not given; therefore, the modern sounds deriving from OE *ēor* in *beer, dear, deer* are listed. Wright says, "The combination *ēor* has gen. become [iə(r, i:r] in such words as *beer, dear, deer*."

There are given here only those districts in Wright's records which lie within the area where *near* 'kidney' is used, that is, where *ear* 'organ of hearing' and *near* 'kidney' could have come into conflict.

District	OE *ēar* in *ear* 'ear'	OE *ēor* in *beer*	*dear*	*deer*
Scotl.		i:r	i:r	i:r
Inv.	iər	iər	iər	iər
Abd.		iər	iər	iər
S.Sc.		iər		
Edb.		i:r	i:r	i:r
Cum. m.	iə	iə	iə	iə
n.		iər	iər	
Wm.	iə		iə	i:r
w.		i:r	i:r	
Nhb.				iə
s.	iə	iə	iə	
se.			iər	
sw.			iər	iər
me.		i:r	i:r	
n.	iər			
Dur.		iə	iə	
n.	iə			iə
Yks.		iə	iə	
nnw.		eiə(r	eiə(r iə(r	
sw.	iə			
Lan.	iə	iə	iə	iə
Stf. n.	ɛə	ɛə	ɛə	ɛə
s.		iə		iə
Linc.		iə	iə	iə
nw.	iə			
Norf.				ɛə
ne.	ɑː	ɛə		
s.	ɛə	ɛə, iə		
Suff. e.		ɛə, iə	ɛə	
Der.		iə		
e.			ɛə	
n.	iə		iə	iə
nw.			iə	iə
Ches. s.		eiə	eiə(r	

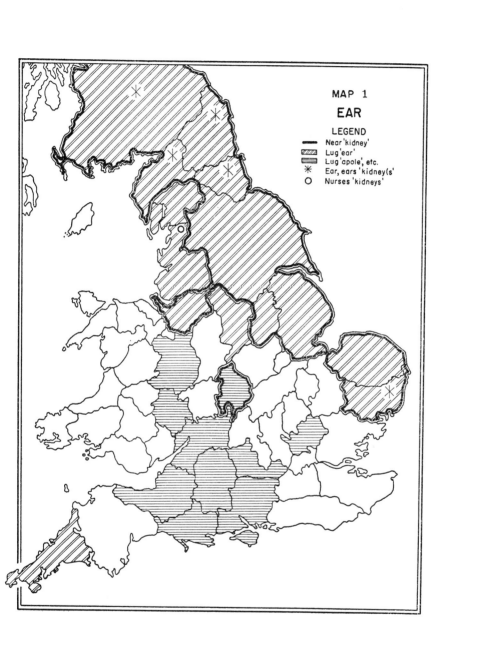

MAP 1

EAR

LEGEND

▬	Near 'kidney'
▨	Lug 'ear'
☰	Lug 'apole', etc.
✳	Ear, ears 'kidney(s'
○	Nurses 'kidneys'

II

Conflict of Gate 'Gateway' and Gate 'Road'

CONFLICT which arose, not in consequence of phonetic change that brought two or more words into homonymy, but as the result of confusion between a native English word and a foreign importation is illustrated in the history of the terms *gate* 'entrance, door, gate' and *gate* 'way, road, path, etc.'

Gate 'entrance, door, opening in a wall, gate' (sb.¹ in *NED*) is derived from OE ȝeat, ȝæt, pl. *gatu*. Words corresponding to it in form are to be found in other Germanic languages—ON *gat* 'opening, passage'; OS *gat* 'eye of a needle,' which gave LG and Du. *gat* 'gap, hole, breach'; OFris. *gat* 'hole, opening'; no representative in Gothic and HG. The declension in OE "was *gæt, gætes, gæte* in the sing., and *gatu, -a, -um* in the plur., according to the phonetic law by which *a* became *æ* cxc. when a back vowel followed in the next syllable" (*NED*). Singular and plural forms developed in different directions; "the g (= γ)," the *NED* continues, "before *æ* became palatalized, and the influence of the palatal ȝ caused the change of *æ* into *ea*. Hence the stem assumed the two forms ȝeat- and *gat-*, which are respectively represented by the α [forms in ȝ-, y-, etc.] and β [forms in ga-] types in the later language." The two did not long remain restricted to singular and plural respectively, but were used interchangeably until gradually *gat-* forms prevailed in the literary language. The *NED* tells us, and we know from other sources later to be discussed in detail, that the forms arising from the palatalized ȝ were prevalent in Middle English in the North and North and West Midland districts and in the Southwest, and are today in frequent use dialectally in the same regions and occasionally elsewhere. *Gat-* forms, from the original plural, prevailed elsewhere and by the 16th century had become the only forms in literary, or Standard English. Various causes may have operated to strengthen the hold of *gat-*, as opposed to ȝat-, ȝeat-, yat-, in the standard language—frequent use of the word in the plural, perhaps, or influence of the corresponding ON *gat* 'opening, passage' on the English term, or general Scandinavian influence in English on words in g-, such as *give*, lending support to the forms with unpalatalized g-.

But the survival of the forms with palatalized ȝ- in dialects of the present day immediately suggests further questions. Why, if Scandinavian influence operating to secure the dominance of g- forms is responsible for the exclusive presence of *gate* [geit] in Standard English, should *yate*, etc. [jeit, etc.] be the common dialectal spelling and pronunciation of the word in the North and North and West Midlands, just where Scandinavian influence would exert itself most strongly? The history of the second word *gate*, meaning 'way, road, path, street; journey, manner of going; manner, method,' is involved in the answer to this and other such questions.

Gate (sb.² in *NED*) 'way, road, street, etc.' is first recorded in English about the year 1200. It was adopted from ON *gata*, with the same meanings (cf. OHG *gazza*, MnG *gasse* 'lane'). It became firmly established in English, especially in the Northern and North Midland districts and in Scotland. But it is now current in Standard English in only one sense; *gait*, a spelling which appeared first in the 15th century and which after two centuries of use among Scottish and northern writers became the generally accepted spelling of the word in this sense, means 'manner of walking or stepping, bearing or carriage while moving, walk.' The other less specialized meanings—'way, road, street'—and the various more or less specific senses grouped in the *NED* under 'act of going' are to be found today only in dialect and in place-names. The position of the two words in English may be presented briefly thus: *gate* 'road, street' is a common term in a large section of England, northern for the most part, but did not make for itself a permanent place in Standard English; *gate* 'entrance, gate' is a widely used word both in Standard English and in dialect, appearing in the dialects of the North and North and West Midlands, to a great extent, in the variant spelling and pronunciation *yate* [jeit].

This situation is, must be, the result of conflict between homonyms. Standard English did not admit two terms identical in sound with meanings so evidently capable of confusion as 'gate' and 'way, road, street.' *The town gate*, a common term for the chief village street in parts of north England, would easily be misinterpreted by those to whom *gate* 'entrance' was a familiar term. "He took the gate toward N-" has two possible meanings. The brief anecdote related in Haigh's study of the Huddersfield dialect illustrates, in a mildly amusing way, the possibility of confusion. It is given in connection with *agate* [əgeit],¹ a derivative of *gate* 'way, act of going, etc.' with the modified senses 'agoing, on the way, on the move, in action, at work':

A southern gentleman, recently come to reside in this district, was listening to a charwoman in his house telling a woeful tale of poverty—her son and daughter were ill and unable to work, "ən' if," she said, "mi uzbənd worn't kīpin əgēt, au duən't nō wæt wi shẹd dū." "Why," exclaimed the gentleman innocently, "and is your husband a *gate-keeper*, Mrs. Booth?"

1. Haigh, *A New Glossary of the Dialect of the Huddersfield District*, under *əgēt*. Haigh's phonetic notation is used in the quotation.

Speakers were forced, to express it thus, to choose between the two. The OE word fulfilled a genuine need in the language. Even now there is no simple synonym for *gate: barrier* is more extended, *door* more limited in meaning. The French word for 'gate,' *porte* (from Lat. *porta* 'door, gate'), existed already in English but was itself subject to confusion with OE *port* 'haven, harbor' from Lat. *portus*, and by the 14th century was more or less generally restricted to the meaning 'gate or gateway of a city or walled town,' in which sense it is still in use in Scotland. It is not surprising that *gate*, from OE ȝeat-, *gat-*, held its own in the standard language against the ON derivative, with its synonyms *way, road, path, street*. But *gate* 'road' was not, as we have seen, entirely vanquished. It survives as a widely used dialect word. And the forms that the two quite generally assume in dialect offer the strongest support for the theory of conflict as the determining factor in their present status.

Gate 'a way, road, street' is preëminently a Northern and North Midland word, though it appears also to some extent in the Southwest. The records in Wright's *English Dialect Dictionary* show it in common use in Scotland, Cumberland, Northumberland, Durham, Westmorland, Yorkshire, Lancashire, and in Cheshire, Derbyshire, Nottinghamshire, Lincolnshire, with sporadic appearances elsewhere.[2] It occurs in several southern counties, Cornwall, Devon, Somerset, Wiltshire, Hampshire, but not commonly in the sense 'road, street, way.' In the case of 'trick, habit,' meanings recorded in these southern districts, confusion with *gate* 'entrance' was not likely. The instance that Wright offers for Oxfordshire is a place-name, *Barnard Gate*, and probably involves an error.[3] On the map for this study (Map 2) the areas in which, according to Wright's records, *gate* 'road, street, path, way' appears with any degree of frequency are indicated.

If imminent confusion with the homonym *gate* 'entrance, door' did operate to debar *gate* 'street' from Standard English and to limit it to dialect, we should expect to find that the two do not exist side by side, unchanged, in the same dialect. And it is here that the various records of dialect become most interesting.

The *English Dialect Dictionary* does not give in detail the pronunciation of *gate* 'entrance' in each separate community or county. It is possible that some of the forms spelled with *g-* are pronounced [j]. But the *y-* forms are conclusive evidence of the palatalized *g-*,

2. The space devoted to this word, in its various senses, in the *EDD* is almost seven columns, more if various derivatives are considered, such as *agate, nogate*, etc.

3. Henry Alexander, in *The Place-Names of Oxfordshire, Their Origin and Development*, Oxford, 1912, gives as the source of the name OE *geat*. In view of the fact that the name is, according to evidence that he offers, pronounced as though spelled *Barnut Yat*, this is probably the true source rather than *gate* 'road.'

from OE ʒeat-, ʒæt-, and indicate a pronunciation different from that of *gate,* from ON *gata.* And the *y-* forms appear with great consistency in the northern counties, in an area almost coincident with that already indicated for *gate* 'street.' Wright records them in the *English Dialect Dictionary* and in the *English Dialect Grammar* in Scotland, Northumberland, Durham, Cumberland, Westmorland, Lancashire, Yorkshire, Cheshire, Derbyshire, Lincolnshire, Rutlandshire, Leicestershire, Oxfordshire (part), Worcestershire, Shropshire (to some extent), Wiltshire, Herefordshire, north Staffordshire, in parts of Northamptonshire and Gloucestershire, in Cornwall and Devon, and occasionally elsewhere (see area indicated on the map). In this area [j]-forms are not found to the entire exclusion of [g]-forms; especially in the southernmost counties of the northern group [g] and [gj]-forms[4] are frequently found, indicating dialectal wavering between the two types. But the very fact that the areas in which these [j]-forms appear are so nearly coincident with the *gate* 'street' area is striking in its suggestion of the forces at work in bringing about this particular situation.

Wright's records may be supplemented by numerous others that point to this same separation of the two words by the retention of the normally developed form of OE ʒeat 'gate,' with palatalized ʒ-. Haigh's work on the Huddersfield dialect indicates confusion between the two, [geit] and [jeit] being given for both.[5] The same confusion is apparent in this section of Yorkshire in Wright's records,[6] and in place-names of that approximate vicinity. Haigh, however, gives for most *derivatives* of *gate* (from ON *gata*) pronunciations with [g]: [əgeit], [əgeitərdz], [geitərdz].[7]

But in various other records of dialect for particular sections such confusion is not indicated. In Jamieson's *Scottish Dictionary, gait, gate* means 'street, way, road, etc.' and is a common, much-used word, the space allotted to it in the *Dictionary* being almost three columns long; *gatelins, gateward, gatewards,* adverbs, mean 'straight, or directly, in the way towards.' Yet, *yett, yhate, yete* are the only forms given of the word meaning 'gate.' *Yett-cheek* means 'the side or post of the gate'; *yethouse* is 'a gate-house.' In the *Supplement* we find *gett,* sb., a form of *gait* 'a road, way'; *common-gett* 'highway, public road, street, causeway'; and *yate* 'gate,' *yate-cheek, yate-stoop* 'the post or side of a gate.'

---

4. See Wright, *English Dialect Grammar,* Oxford, London, 1905.
5. Haigh's symbols are [gēt] and [yēt].
6. *Yate* is given as a form of *gate* 'road, street' in west Yorkshire and in Northumberland.
7. Haigh's symbols: [ẹgēt], [ẹgētẹrdz], [gētẹrdz]. There is one exception: [yētẹrdz] is given as well as [gētẹrdz].

Sir Allen Mawer, in his study of the place-names of Northumberland and Durham, indicates that the prevailing dialectal pronunciation of *gate* 'gate, gateway' in those counties is [jɑt, jet, jĭt], though he does not state that this is exclusively the case.[8]

Sir Alfred Pease in his *Dictionary of the Dialect of the North Riding of Yorkshire*,[9] gives similar records. *Gate, gait, geeat* mean 'way, road, direction, street.' He gives them as words which have "been in COMMON use (general or local) between 1867 and 1927, the period of the author's familiarity with the dialect,"[10] and devotes almost a column in the dictionary to illustration and comment upon them. One comment is significant of the possible confusion between this word and English *gate* 'gate' and of the consequent shifting in the forms of place-names to be noted in many northern districts:

The older roads and streets in the North are "gates" . . . i.e., ways. Many people suppose the names of streets, say in York and the larger towns are derived from the names of the Gates in the walls, or from gateways, but the reverse is the case where any gateways remain. In York the Micklegate gives its name to the Bar or Gate in the city wall, the same with Walmgate Bar or Fishergate Postern, &c.

And *yat* is the form in which the word meaning 'gate' appears, also indicated as a common word in the dialect:

Yat, sb. (C[ommon]) A gate; Pl. *Yats* (also formerly *Yates*); also anciently 'a way.' The common term for all kinds of gates, not confined to Yorkshire but common also in Durham, Cumberland and Westmorland. (A.S. *Geat, Gat.*)

Subsequent entries under *yat* are also of interest:

Oweryat, sb. (C.) A stile, but applied usually to steps over stone walls. *Huntyats, bridleyats, wicketyats* are the smaller hand-gates for horsemen and pedestrians. The word is common in place and field-names. *Chop Yat* (Bilsdale) is now, to suit the P.O., often written and printed Chop Gate; as *Aysdale Yat* has become Aysdale Gate.

A *yatcrewk* is the iron hook on which the ring of a gate-hinge works; a *yathoos* is a gatehouse; a *yatsneck* the iron catch on a gate; a *yat-*

8. Allen Mawer, *The Place-Names of Northumberland and Durham, Cambridge Archaeological and Ethnological Series*, Cambridge, 1920. The pronunciation is given by him as [jɑt, jet, je·t, jĭt], [j] representing the sound of *y* in *yet*, and [a] representing the "North Country *a*": see p. 261, § 33. See also p. 230: "O.E. *geat* = 'gate.' This should give North. and Sc. dialectal *yet*. Modern forms in *gate* are due to the O.E. pl. form *gatu* and to the influence of the word *gate* = road . . ."; and p. 269: "In Eastgate, Hooker Gate, Leadgate, Portgate, Stotgate, Westgate there has been confusion between *gate* (Dial. *yet*), an opening, and *gate*, a road."
9. *Op. cit.*, pp. 49, 48, 160, under *Gate, Gait, Yat*, etc.
10. *Ibid.*, p. xx, explanation of the symbol "C."

stead is a gateway, the place for a gate. No [g]-forms for this word are recorded. In this section of Yorkshire the two words *gate* are, beyond doubt, kept formally distinct.

Other records are similar, though as a rule less detailed. Among "provincialisms" of East Yorkshire appear *gait* (vulg. *geeat*) 'street,' *gait* 'a way,' and *yat* 'a gate,' *yathouse* 'a high carriage-gateway through a building.' There are no [g]-forms for 'gate.'[11]

In *A List of Ancient Words at Present Used in the Mountainous District of the West Riding of Yorkshire*, compiled by Robert Willan, are the entries: "*Gate*, sb. a street or road," and "*Yate* (pronounced *yett*) sb. a gate to a farmyard, a close, or common."[12]

In Ray's list of North-Country Words, 1691, *gate* is 'a way or path,' *yate* is 'a gate.' Neither word is given in his collection of "South and East-Countrey Words."[13]

Children in Scotland today "swing on the yett all day," and travelers in Lancashire and other parts of the North hear the request, "Please sneck the yett (Please fasten the gate)."[14]

Such records might be cited at length. The conclusion becomes more and more evident, on investigation, that in the dialects of the counties in which the ON *gate* 'road, street' is a living term, the native *gate* 'opening, entrance, gate' has been preserved in forms not homonymous with the other, that is, forms with palatalized 3- as opposed to the Standard English *gate*, to an extent which is not true in other sections where there was little or no interference from the ON derivative.

Studies in place-names offer closely parallel evidence. Difficulties are numerous in handling such material: records, both geographical and historical, are still far from complete; some editors of place-name studies are satisfied with grouping names in *Gate-* or *-gate*, from both sources, together; the element of time must constantly be taken into consideration. But, used with caution, place-names offer evidence of the same prevailing tendency to avoid confusion between the two terms by keeping them distinct in form and pronunciation.

Gate as an element in place-names, principally as suffix, is frequent throughout England. Investigations reveal, as we should expect, that names in which this component is to be traced to ON *gata* 'road, street, way' are prevailingly northern. They appear in Scotland, in

---

11. W. H. Marshall, *Provincialisms of East Yorkshire*, English Dialect Society, Series B, Reprinted Glossaries ed. by W. W. Skeat, Part I, No. 2, London, 1873.

12. Robert Willan, *A List of Ancient Words at Present Used in the Mountainous District of the West Riding of Yorkshire*, English Dialect Society, Series B, Reprinted Glossaries ed. by W. W. Skeat, Part I, No. 7, London, 1873.

13. John Ray, *Collection of North-Country Words*, and *Collection of 'South and East-Countrey Words*,' English Dialect Society, Series B, Reprinted Glossaries ed. by W. W. Skeat, Nos. 15 and 16, London, 1874.

14. Oral sources of information.

Cumberland, Westmorland, Durham, Yorkshire, Lancashire, Derbyshire, Lincolnshire, Northamptonshire, Huntingdonshire, and (?) Shropshire. Names like *Barkgate* in Cumberland, *Scattergate* in Westmorland, *Cowgate* (Newcastle-on-Tyne), *Ridgate* in Lancashire, *Galgate* in Lancashire (meaning " 'the Galloway Road,' cattle drovers from Galloway having given name to the road on which the place stands"[15]), *Kirkhamgate* in southwest Yorkshire, *Gate Helmsley* in north Yorkshire are numerous. Further investigation will probably show them in neighboring counties as well. This area agrees closely with that already indicated for *gate* 'street' as an independent word. What form in this same area does *-gate* of OE origin assume? This is the question of immediate concern.

Both *-gate* and *-yate, -yett*, etc. forms appear. But beneath that superficial observation are to be discovered certain significant points. To begin with, names containing this element *-gate,* from OE *geat-, gat-*, are considerably more numerous in the South than in the North. Where *gate* meant 'road' and 'street' and was so used in numerous place-names and street- and road-names, *gate* meaning 'gate, gateway' was not so frequently utilized in the formation of names as in other sections where it alone appeared. But the spelling in the areas where the two are used together is of greater significance than the question of distribution. In the South (except in Devon) *-gate* is well-nigh the universal spelling. A few names with *-yate* occur, as for example *Newyatt* in Oxfordshire,[16] *Markyate* now in Hertfordshire,[17] *Bagshot* (from *Baggan get*) now in Wiltshire.[18] But most of these names have the *-gate* suffix. In the Northern and North Midland counties, however, the *-yate* forms predominate, and have predominated, apparently, through centuries. Gradually, standardizing tendencies have changed numerous *-yate* names to the *-gate* that is more in accord with accepted English usage. Confusion with *gate* 'street' is also, no doubt, responsible for some changes from *-yate* to *-gate:* in place-names the original significance of the components is generally lost sight of in time, and confusion between the homonyms might well lead, in this case, to interchange of forms. Thus both influences, that of Standard English *gate* 'gate' and that of *gate* 'street,' here, would tend in time to introduce *-gate* forms. But in spite of such tendencies *-yate* forms persist, are, indeed, somewhat more numerous in these northern areas than the *-gate* forms for the same word. The whole trend is toward a differentiation of English *gate* and

15. Eilert Ekwall, *The Place-Names of Lancashire, Publications of the University of Manchester,* No. 149, English Series, No. 11, Manchester, 1922. See under *Galgate,* p. 170.
16. Alexander, *The Place-Names of Oxfordshire.*
17. W. W. Skeat, *The Place-Names of Bedfordshire,* Cambridge Antiquarian Society, Octavo Publ., No. 42, Cambridge and London, 1906.
18. F. M. Stenton, *The Place-Names of Berkshire* (Reading, 1911), pp. 5, 43.

Old Norse *gate,* and the place-names follow the dialectal trend.
A list of names comprising *gate, yate* (from OE *geat*) from the
counties where -*gate,* from ON *gata,* is frequently a component of
place-names will, perhaps, demonstrate most clearly and economically
the form that the native English word takes in the areas where possible homonymy was a factor in determining that form:[19]

Cumberland:[20]	*Yeathouse*
Northumberland and Durham:[21]	*Eastgate,* in 1637 *Eastyat*
	Hooker Gate, in 1611 *Howkeryeat*
	Leadgate, in 1613 *Lidyate*
	Portgate, in 1382 *Porteyete*
	Stotgate, in 1446 *le Stotyate*
	Westgate, in 1457 *Westyatshele*
	Wingate
Westmorland.[20]	(None listed)

Lancashire (Wyld):[22] *Lidiate*
Butt Yeats, Wray
Hang Yeats, Lanc.
Pott Yeats, Caton
Water Yeat, B-in-F.
Yates, Garstang
Wingates (and some fifteen others with
-*gate,* for which particular origins are
not given, some obviously to be con-
nected with *gate* 'road').

Lancashire (Ekwall):[23] *Yate Bank*
Lydiate
Water Yeat
Wingates,   in 1272 *Windyatis*
in 1451 *lee Wyndzates*
Haggate
Gathurst

19. The list is based upon material in the works on place-names mentioned by
name, which material may not be complete in every case. The general proportion is
probably fairly accurate.
20. W. J. Sedgefield, *The Place-Names of Cumberland and Westmorland, Publications of the University of Manchester,* No. 98, English Series, No. 7, Manchester, 1915.
21. Mawer, *The Place-Names of Northumberland and Durham.*
22. Henry Cecil Wyld, in collaboration with T. Oakes Hirst, *The Place Names of
Lancashire,* London, 1911.
23. Ekwall, *The Place-Names of Lancashire.*

SW. Yorkshire:[24]   *Lidyate*
                    Lidget,   in 1379 *Lydeyate*
                    Lidgate,   in 1514 *Lidyate*
                    Yateholme, Holmfirth, "has for its prefix a common form of the OE. *geat,* a gate."

North Riding of
    Yorkshire:[25]   *Yatts*
                    Lidyyate Way
                    Waitgate, earlier *Thwaiteʒate*

In Northamptonshire, in the same hundred in the extreme northeast of the county appear *Deeping Gate* "the 'gate' or road to Deeping"; *Normangate Field,* with *-gate* probably from ON *gata,* and *Pilsgate,* in which *-gate* is from OE *geat* and for which there seems to have been considerable hesitation between *-gate* and *-yate,* the name appearing as *Pyllesyate* in 1364 and in 1478, as *Pyllysate* in 1517, and *Pyliate* in 1558. The same hesitation is to be noted in the various records of *Bozeat,* in a more southern hundred. The long period of uncertainty over the form of the name is, perhaps, significant of confusion between the two words *gate.*[26]

The evidence from place-names is not conclusive, in part because of the incompleteness of records and in part because of the strong standardizing influences at work upon them which would not affect the simple word in the same way. But the large number of *-yate* forms among the names of the North (and in the extreme Southwest, where *gate* 'road, way' is known[27]), especially in contrast to the small number of such forms in the southeastern counties, e.g., Middlesex, Surrey, Sussex,[28] is indicative of the tendency to differentiate the two words which were otherwise homonyms.

A further source of evidence is to be found in Middle English writ-

24. Armitage Goodall, *Place-Names of South-West Yorkshire, That Is, Of So Much of the West Riding as Lies South of the Aire from Keighley Onwards,* Cambridge, 1914. See pp. 144, 172, etc.

25. A. H. Smith, *The Place-Names of the North Riding of Yorkshire,* English Place-Name Society, v, Cambridge, 1928.

26. J. E. B. Gover, A. Mawer, and F. M. Stenton, *The Place-Names of Northamptonshire,* English Place-Name Society, x, Cambridge, 1933. See pp. 234, 233, 231, etc.

27. See, for example, *Yate, Yeat, Yeatt, Yetland(s, Yettington, Boreat, Buckyett, Ditchett, Horsyeat, Lidyates Barn,* listed among the names of Devon: J. E. B. Gover, A. Mawer, and F. M. Stenton, *The Place-Names of Devon,* English Place-Name Society, VIII and IX, Cambridge, 1931 and 1932. See p. 663 under *geat* and p. 665 under *hlidgeat.*

28. J. E. B. Gover, *The Place Names of Middlesex,* London, 1922; J. E. B. Gover, A. Mawer, and F. M. Stenton, in collaboration with A. Bonner, *The Place-Names of Surrey,* English Place-Name Society, XI, Cambridge, 1934; A. Mawer and F. M. Stenton, with the assistance of J. E. B. Gover, *The Place-Names of Sussex,* English Place-Name Society, VI and VII, Cambridge, 1929 and 1930; other volumes of the English Place-Name Society publications and other general works on place-names.

ings representing various dialects. To a striking extent the words *gate* 'street, way, road' and *gate* 'gate' (in the forms *yate, ʒat, ʒeat,* etc.) are kept distinct.

Barbour's *The Bruce,*[29] dating from the 14th century, has *gat* 'way, road, passage' and *ʒat, ʒet* 'gate, gateway':

> "Ilk man a syndri gat is gane." (VI.577)

> "Thai sparit [closed and fastened] the ʒettis hastely
> And in hy to the vallis [walls] ran." (VI.444–5)

> "And the portar, that saw hym weill
> Cum neir the ʒat, It opnyt soyn.
> And than bwnnok, forouten hoyn,
> Gert call the wayn deliuerly;
> And quhen it [wes] set evinly
> Betuix the chekys of the ʒet,
> Swa that men mycht It spar na gat,
> He cryit. . . ." (X.224–31)

In the Jacob play and the Second Shepherds' Play in the Towneley cycle of miracle plays,[30] representing the dialect of southwest Yorkshire of the 14th century probably, occur *gate* meaning 'going, path,' *gaytt-door* 'street-door,' and *yate* 'gate.'

> "[Deus.] Iacob, have thou no kyns drede!
>   I shall the clethe, I shall the fede.
>   Whartfull [safe and sound] shall I make thi gate. . . ."
>   (Page 52, lines 27–9)

> "Iacob A! lord! what may this mene?
>   what have I herd in slepe, and sene?
>   That god leynyd hym to a stegh [ladder],
>   And spake to me, it is no leghe;
>   And now is here none othere gate,
>   bot godis howse and heuens yate."
>   (Page 53, lines 35 ff.)

> "Mak Then myght I be tane,/that were a cold swette!
>   Go spar
>   The gaytt door."
>   (Page 126, lines 326 ff.)

29. John Barbour, *The Bruce,* EETS, Extra Series, XI, London, 1870; XXI, London, 1874; XXIX, London, 1877; LV, London, 1889.
30. George England and Alfred W. Pollard, eds., *The Towneley Plays,* EETS, Extra Series, LXXI, 1897.

In *Sir Gawayne and The Green Knight*,[31] written in the dialect of the Northwest Midlands of the late 14th century, occur *gate, gates* meaning 'way(s, road(s, path(s' and ӡateӡ 'gates':[32]

"þenne gedereӡ he to Gryngolet with þe gilt heleӡ,
& he ful chauncely hatӡ chosen to þe chef gate,
þat broӡt bremly þe burne to þe bryge ende,
        in haste;
þe bryge watӡ breme vp-brayde,
þe ӡateӡ wer stoken faste,
þe walleӡ were wel arayed,
Hit dut no wyndeӡ blaste."
                                   (ii.xii.777 ff.)

"þe knyӡt tok gates straunge,
In mony a bonk vnbene. . . ."
                                   (ii.ix.709–10)

"The brygge watӡ brayde doun, ðe brode ӡateӡ
Vn barred, & born open, vpon boþe halue. . . ."
                                   (iv.iv.2069–70)

In the *Cursor Mundi*, "a Northumbrian Poem of the XIVth Century,"[33] the differentiation is made unmistakably clear. *Gat, gate, gatt, gatte, gait* all occur for 'way, road, path,' whereas the word meaning 'gate' appears in the forms *yate, yatte, yatt, ӡate, ӡatte*, pl. *yates, ӡates. Yateward* means 'porter, gatekeeper.' Lines 8958 ff. and 1263–4, of the Cotton MS., show the two in juxtaposition:[34]

"Quen þat sco to þe cite com
Sco com in at þat ilk yatte,
þar þis tre lai in hir gatt. . . ."

"þe falau slogh [fallow path] sal be þi gate
O paradis right to þe yate."

Just as clear is the separation of the terms in *A Yorkshire Dialogue in Its Pure Natural Dialect; as it is now commonly spoken in the North Parts of Yorkshire*, by G[eorge] M[eriton]: 1684:[35]

31. Richard Morris, ed., *Sir Gawayne and The Green Knight*, EETS, Orig. Ser., iv, London, 1864; re-edited by Sir Israel Gollancz, EETS, Orig. Ser., ccx, London, 1940 (for 1938).
32. See lines 696, 778, 930, 709; and lines 782, 2069.
33. Richard Morris, ed., *Cursor Mundi*, EETS, Orig. Ser., lvii, London, 1874; lix, London, 1875; lxii, London, 1876; lxvi, London, 1877; lxviii, London, 1878; xcix, London, 1892.
34. See glossary for references. Lines 8958 ff. occur in Vol. lvii, Pt. 2, p. 516; lines 1263–4 in Vol. lvii, Pt. 1, p. 80.
35. W. W. Skeat, ed., *Nine Specimens of English Dialects*, English Dialect Society, No. 76, London, 1896. See p. 163 and Key, where *owse* means 'ox'; *yat* 'gate'; *town-gate* 'the town-street.'

"Yonders our Owse, is loppen o're the Yate;
Nan, Slate him back, as thou gangs up'th Town-gate."
(Lines 353–4)

In the *Ormulum*, in the dialect of Lincolnshire of about 1200;[36] in the poems of John Audelay, in the Northwest Midland dialect of the 15th century;[37] in the poem *Purity*, in the West Midland dialect of the latter half of the 14th century[38] the word *gate* meaning 'way, road' is written *gate*, while *gate* from OE *geat* is written with the ӡ that is, in these texts and frequently throughout Middle English, the symbol for the palatalized *g*. The consistency with which the two words are kept distinct, phonetically, is striking.

Standard English, to repeat, did not admit the two terms, identical in sound and with meanings capable of confusion. *Gate* 'gate' is a wide-spread substantive; *gate* 'way, road, street' is not found, except in the special and derivative sense 'manner of walking, etc.' And dialects as well refuse to admit the terms as homophones. Where *gate* 'street' maintains itself in English, that is, in the Northern and North Midland counties and in the Southwest, chiefly Devon, the native word meaning 'gate, entrance' survives in the form which was the normal descendant of the OE word in the singular but which did not become the accepted form in Standard English. Hence, in areas where the ON word still lives, we find in dialects of the present day, in place-names, and in documents representing Middle English of various sections, *yate* [jeit] and forms phonetically similar as the prevailing dialectal type of the native English word. These *yate* forms appear in other areas as well, where the influence of Standard English has not fully penetrated, but not extensively or frequently. *Gate* is the accepted form in these areas, as in Standard English. And *gate* from ON *gata* does not appear together with it.

36. Robert Holt, ed., *The Ormulum*, Oxford, 1878.
37. Ella K. Whiting, ed., *The Poems of John Audelay*, EETS, Orig. Ser., CLXXXIV, London, 1931 (for 1930).
38. Robert J. Menner, ed., *Purity, A Middle English Poem, Yale Studies in English*, LXI, New Haven and London, 1920.

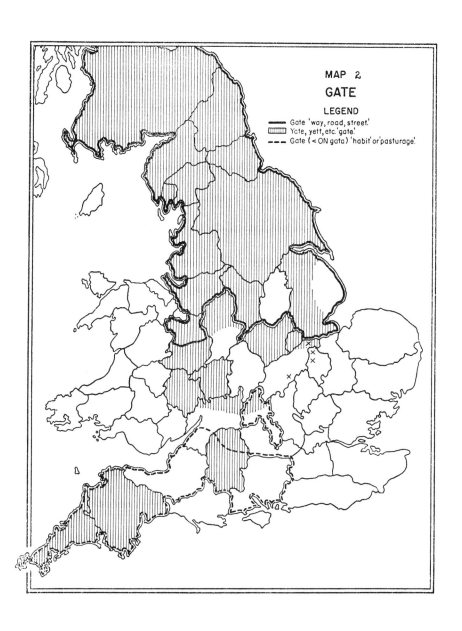

MAP 2

GATE

LEGEND
Gate 'way, road, street.'
Yate, yett, etc. 'gate.'
Gate (< ON gata) 'habit' or 'pasturage'.

III

Conflicts Involving ME ę̄ and ME ẹ̄

OE ǣ (from WGmc. *ai* + *i*)[1]
OE (Sax.) ǣ (from WGmc. ā)[2]
OE *ēa*[3]
OE *e* in open syllable[4]
OE *eo* in open syllable[5]
OF *e* and *ai*[6]

} became ME ę̄

THE group of sound-changes represented in this general way affected an untold number of words in the English vocabulary and brought into homonymy numerous sets of words that had before been quite independent of one another, phonetically as well as semantically. OE *lǣdan* 'to lead,' for example, and OE *lēad* 'lead, a metal' both became ME *lę̄d(e;* OE *lēaf(e* 'permission' and OE *lǣfan* 'to leave' became ME *lę̄v(e;* OE *teran* 'to rend' and OE *tēar* 'a tear' became ME *tę̄r(e,* etc. This list might be extended indefinitely. A glance at the three examples cited, representative as they are of many words still extant in English, will show that no inconvenience arose from their likeness in sound for speakers or writers who used them. This was true, perhaps, in the greater number of cases, homonymy (as has been stated fully elsewhere) in and of itself offering no resistance to the continued existence of words.

But there were certain instances in which confusion did arise as the result of homonymy. When OE *hǣlan* 'to heal' and OE *helan* 'to cover, to hide' both became ME *hę̄le;* when OE *lēan* 'reward, gift' and OE *lǣn* 'loan' became ME *lę̄n;* when OE *lēas* 'falsehood' and OF *lais, leis,* AF *les* 'a legal contract' became ME *lę̄s* confusion was only to be expected. Examples of the conflict of homonyms, because of the variety and complexity of all the factors involved, must to a great extent be studied separately; but in this instance several may be grouped loosely together, since one ME sound, long open ę̄, is involved in each.

i. Lean and Its Homonyms

The substantive *loan* and the verb *lend* are common words among English-speaking people. But neither exists today in the form that

1. Jordan, *Handbuch*, §§ 47, 48: ǣ > ę̄ in 12th century.
2. *Ibid.*, §§ 47, 49: ǣ > ę̄ in 12th century.
3. *Ibid.*, § 81: *ēa* > ǣ (about 1000) > ę̄ (12th century).
4. *Ibid.*, § 33.3: *e* in open syllable > ę̄ in 13th century.
5. *Ibid.*, § 73: *eo* > ę̄ (12th and 14th centuries).   6. *Ibid.*, § 225 and § 233.

would normally represent the OE source-words. *Loan* is an ON borrowing of the 13th century; *lend* is a Middle English development, not strictly etymological, of OE *lænan*. The history of the two offers an example of phonetic confusion in late Old English or early Middle English times.

OE *Læn* and OE *Lēan*

OE *læn* meant 'a loan, a grant, a gift'; in connection with land, 'a grant that may be recalled, a lease.' It is cognate with OHG *lēhan*, ON *lān*,[7] all from Gmc. *laihwniz-, -oz-*. The *æ* is, accordingly, Common OE (exc. Kent.) and would have, or did, become *ē*[εː] about 1100: hence *lēn* 'a loan, a grant, a lease.' There is little evidence that the word survived into Middle English.[8] As early as the middle of the 13th century its place is taken by *lan(e, lon(e*—ME *lān(e, lǫn(e* [lɑːnə, lɔːnə]; later [loun]—a form taken from the ON cognate *lān*, with the same meanings; it was taken into Middle English early enough to have shared the Southern and Midland change of OE *ā* into EME *ǭ*.

It seems highly probable, especially in the light of the history of the corresponding verbs, that phonetic identity of two native English substantives was a major factor bringing about the substitution of ON *lān* for OE *læn*. The second word is OE *lēan*, which had also become *lēn* [lεːn] in the 12th century;[9] this word meant 'a reward, a gift, compensation, remuneration,' sometimes 'loan.' It came into Middle English in the senses 'reward, recompense' and appears in records until about 1250. Between homonymous words, one meaning 'a loan, a grant, a lease' and the other 'reward, recompense,' confusion was certain.[10] Both substantives went out of use. *Lēn(e* 'a loan' was replaced by *lān(e*, later *loan*, from Old Norse. *Lēn(e* 'a reward' lived until about 1250; in the early 14th century appears first (according to records of the *NED*) the synonym *reward*, somewhat later *recompense*, both from French, which have taken over, in Modern English, the functions of the native word.

OE *Lænan*, OE *Lēanian*, and OE *Lēan*

The history of the corresponding verbs supplements in an illuminating way that of the substantives and makes more convincing the

---

7. See Holthausen, *Altenglisches etymologisches Wörterbuch.*

8. The word *leane* appears as a variant form of *lane* (i.e., *loan*) in MS. T. of *Sawles Warde*. Cf. *NED, Loan*, sb.[1], 1.*a* 1240 quot.

9. Jordan, *Handbuch*, § 81.

10. Hemken's suggestion (*Das Aussterben alter Substantiva*, p. 35) that *lean* 'reward' conflicted with *hlæne* 'thin' and in consequence went out of use can scarcely be supported, since there is little real likelihood of confusion between words used so differently as are those two.

probability of the direct influence of homonymy upon both verbs and substantives.

OE *lēanian,* meaning 'to reward, recompense, repay, requite,' would have become ME **lẹne(n* [lɛ:nə(n] in the 12th century, with the change of *ēa* into *ẹ*. It does not appear in Middle English in the records of the *NED,* though, as has been shown, the corresponding substantive *lean, len* [lɛ:n] 'reward' is recorded until the middle of the 13th century. An earlier writer on the subject[11] gives as the possible cause of its loss phonetic identity with *lẹne* from OE *hlǣnian* 'to grow or make thin.' Confusion here is not very likely, though, perhaps, possible in certain connections. The reason for the disappearance of *lẹne(n* 'to reward' is to be sought, rather, in the history of the verbs *lǣnan* 'to give, grant, lease, lend' and OE *lēan* 'to blame.' *Lǣnan* 'to give' also became ME *lẹne* [lɛ:nə] about the beginning of the 12th century. Its earliest senses carry, almost without exception, the idea of temporary possession of the object concerned, as do related words in OE: *lǣnelic* 'passing, transitory,' *lǣnland* 'leased land,' *lǣne* 'temporary, inconstant, transitory,' etc. Thus conflict with **lẹne(n* 'to reward, to recompense' is more than likely. There is a sentence in Lord Berners' *Chronicles of Froissart*[12] which illustrates well how the two verbs might come into conflict: "So the kynge lende or gaue him, I cannat tell wheder, a lx. thousande frankes." It is obviously essential that the two verbs should be distinguished in sound and form, and speakers and writers would naturally make use of words so distinguished to avoid confusion in sense. *Lēanian* 'to reward' does not appear in Middle English records, though it may have existed in the language early in that period, as the presence of the substantive *lean,* from OE *lēan* 'a reward,' would lead us to surmise; *lǣnan* 'to lend' does appear, but in the 13th century, that is, within a century or so after the time when confusion became possible, it began to be used in the *lend* forms that later became the only recorded forms of the verb.[13] Influence of analogy, given as the explanation of the change, would be strengthened, or itself brought into play, by imminent confusion with the other verb.

And these were not the only possibilities of confusion. OE *lēan* 'to blame,' having become ME **lẹn,* would have met interference

---

11. Offe, *Das Aussterben alter Verba,* p. 26: *"lēanian* 'belohnen' zu *lēan: reward* musste als me. **lēnen* zusammenfallen mit **lēnen* < *hlǣnian* 'mager werden'; es wird vielleicht deswegen das zu dem sb. *reward* gehörende vb. *rewarden* > *to reward* vorgezogen."

12. Quoted here from *NED,* where it is given under *Lend* v.[2]

13. *NED* gives the following explanation of the form *lend:* "The substitution of *lend-* for *lēn-* in the present-stem, which began early in ME., is explained by the fact that the pa. t. *lende* would regularly correspond either to *lēnen* or *lenden* in the infinitive, and the preponderance of analogy (Cf. *Lend* v.[1], also *bend, rend, send, wend*) was on the side of the latter form." *Len, lean* still appear in Sc. and Northern dialect.

from *lēn(e* 'to reward': *Wilt þu lēne him:* 'Blame, reproach him'? Or 'reward him'? Syntactical constructions would, to some extent at least, have distinguished it from *lēn(e* 'to lend.' The verb *lēan,* ME **lēn,* does not appear in Middle English;[14] in the form *bilēan* (from OE *be-lēan*) it appears in a homily of the 12th century,[15] the prefix probably serving to differentiate it from its homonyms and to preserve it in the language for a time. The substitute *blame* (from Old French) begins to appear at the very beginning of the 13th century and very soon, apparently, replaced the native verb entirely.

Such threatened confusion, or, better, actual homonymy between words not all of which have been recorded, may well account for the losses and changes and substitutions in the history of the four thus far discussed.

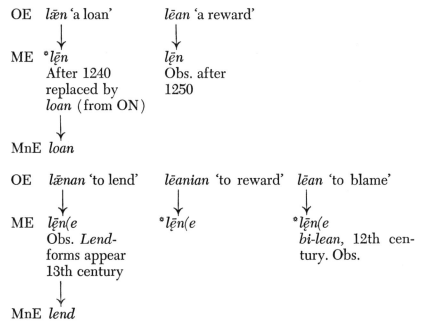

OE   *lǣn* 'a loan'   *lēan* 'a reward'

ME   **lēn*   *lēn*
       After 1240   Obs. after
       replaced by   1250
       loan (from ON)

MnE   *loan*

OE   *lǣnan* 'to lend'   *lēanian* 'to reward'   *lēan* 'to blame'

ME   *lēn(e*   **lēn(e*   **lēn(e*
     Obs. *Lend-*   *bi-lean,* 12th cen-
     forms appear   tury. Obs.
     13th century

MnE   *lend*

In not one of these five cases did the sound-combination *lēn* [lɛːn] survive. But it existed in the language and is represented in Modern Standard English both by verb and adjective, as the next section shows.

OE *Hlǣne* and OE *Lǣne*

OE *hlǣne* became ME *lēn(e,* MnE *lean* 'thin, wanting in flesh.' It is in common use, and has been for centuries. OE *lǣne* meaning 'lent,

14. See F. H. Stratmann, *A Middle-English Dictionary,* Oxford, 1891.
15. Richard Morris, ed., *Old English Homilies of the Twelfth Century* (Second Series), EETS, Orig. Ser., LIII (London, 1873), 107.

temporary, inconstant, transitory; perishable, frail, poor; weak, sinful' was in Old English also a common word; the fact that it does not appear in Middle or Modern English must be attributed to the inevitable confusion that resulted when both adjectives became ME *lēn(e. The lēne years:* 'the transitory years' or 'the years of famine'? *The lēn young man:* 'the thin young man' or 'the weak, sinful young man'? Oberdörffer's suggestion[16] is not adequate to explain the loss of *lēn* 'transitory.' It is placed by him among the adjectives that have become too short ("zu kurz und undeutlich geworden sind") to convey their meaning clearly and, he says, "vor dem kräftigeren 'transitory' schwindet." *Lēn,* from *læne* 'transitory,' no longer supported by the corresponding substantive *læn* 'loan,' and—a circumstance of greater importance—liable to confusion with another common adjective, went out of use early. *Lean* 'thin' survived.

OE *Hleonian,* OE *Hlænan,* and OE *Hlænian*

Six OE verbs became, or would have become, ME *lēne(n* in the 12th and 13th centuries. Only one of them is to be found in Modern English in the form that normally represents its Old English source.

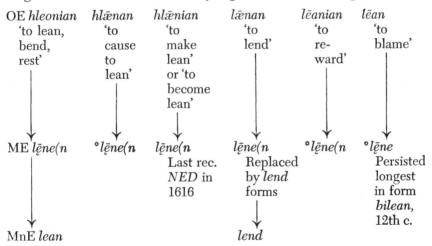

OE *hleonian* 'to lean, bend, rest'	*hlænan* 'to cause to lean'	*hlænian* 'to make lean' or 'to become lean'	*lænan* 'to lend'	*lēanian* 'to reward'	*lēan* 'to blame'
ME *lēne(n*	*lēne(n*	*lēne(n* Last rec. *NED* in 1616	*lēne(n* Replaced by *lend* forms	*lēne(n*	*lēne* Persisted longest in form *bilean,* 12th c.
MnE *lean*			*lend*		

Three of these have already been discussed, *lænan* 'to lend,' *lēanian* 'to reward,' and *lēan* 'to blame.' Among those three interference was likely and probably occurred. And it is possible that the fact that the sound *lēn* [lɛ:n] was common to two, or three, other verbs as well as to these three, though mutual conflict between all six was not likely, hastened the loss of *lēanian* and *lēan* and the change of *lænan* into *lend.*

Of the other three, *hlænan* 'to cause to lean' can be dismissed

16. Oberdörffer, *Das Aussterben altenglischer Adjektive,* pp. 11–12.

quickly. If it survived into Middle English at all it has been absorbed by the verb *to lean*, from *hleonian*. OE *hleonian* with the unrounding of *eo* into *e* (Jordan, §§ 65, 73) became *(h)lenen* in time to share the 13th-century lengthening of *e* in open syllables in the greater part of England: hence *lẹn(e* [lɛ:n(ə) 'to recline, lie down, rest'; somewhat later 'to support oneself on, against something, to lean, to bend, etc.' OE *hlǣnian* 'to become lean, to make lean, to starve' also became ME *lẹne* and appears, as *lean*, in records as late as 1616 (cf. *NED, Lean*, v.[2]). It then went out of use. Confusion between it and *lene, lean* 'to recline, to bend' was likely. The man who said "The body lẹnes," or the other who wrote "Of thing that lẹneth the body"[17] would, in all probability, be misunderstood. For the words might mean either 'The body grows lean' or 'The body bends,' 'Of thing that causes the body to grow thin' or 'Of thing that causes the body to bend.' That English keeps the adjective *lean* but not the verb is corroboration of the surmise that conflict with its homonym hastened the disuse of the verb.

The conflict that resulted from identity of sound has undoubtedly played its part in the history of these words. Of the ten that, by normal development, would have become Modern English [li:n], *lean*, adj. and *lean*, v. alone survive. The others either exist in changed forms or have fallen into disuse.

ii. Lease *and Its Homonyms*

Lease, verb, substantive, adjective, has attracted the attention of students of obsolete English words in more than one instance. But the words (to speak of them separately) have never been discussed with any degree of completeness, the historical, the chronological, aspects of their history never having been taken into consideration.

Offe merely lists *lēasian* 'to tell lies,' and *lesan*, dial. *to lease*, 'to gather' in his Glossary.[18] Oberdörffer gives *lēas* 'false' in a list of obsolete adjectives that are related to substantives and verbs also obsolete: *lēas*, that became *lease* 'falsehood,' *lēasian* 'to tell lies,' *lēas*, that became *lease* 'false.'[19] Hemken, concerned only with nouns, lists *lǣs* 'pasture' and *lēas* 'falsehood' and, in rather a brief comment, attributes the loss of the latter to homonymy with *lease*, from OF *lais, leis, les*.[20]

The group of words spelled *lease* involving the idea of 'falseness'

17. *NED, Lean* v.[2], 1450–80 tr. *Secreta Secret.*[2]
18. Offe, *Das Aussterben alter Verba*, p. 73.
19. Oberdörffer, *Das Aussterben altenglischer Adjektive*, p. 37.
20. Hemken, *Das Aussterben alter Substantiva*, Glossary and p. 35: "*leas* hat ae. zwiefache Bedeutung: den allgemeinen Sinn, den die Wurzel auch in andern germ. Sprachen hat, 'los, frei' > Suffix ne. -less, dann die spez. engl. 'falsch,' die sich im adj. und subst. Verwendung erhält bis zum 16s. Der lautliche Zusammenklang mit lease 'Mietvertrag' < afz. lais, leis, les drängt das alte leas zurück, Wörter wie untruth, falsehood, auch eine Ableitg. leasing 'Lüge' treten als Ersatz ein."

is an interesting one. OE *lēas* 'falsehood' became ME *lease,* but is obsolete after the 16th century; OE *lēasian* became ME *lease* 'to tell lies,' and is obsolete also after the 16th century; OE *lēas* 'false' became ME *lease* 'false' (also the suffix -*less* in a different sense), and this adjective is obsolete earlier than either of the preceding, not being recorded according to the *NED* after *c*1450. OE *lēasung* 'lying, deceit' became ME *leasing* and is now obsolete or archaic, except in dialect. The source of all four is to be found in Gmc. *laus-*, one grade in the ablaut series that has given also *lose, loose,* etc.

These four words—*lēas* 'falsehood,' *lēasian* 'to tell lies,' *lēas* 'false,' *lēasung* 'deceit'—with all the others related closely to them in Old English, are now not used in Standard English. Only one of them, *leasing* 'falsehood,' is known even in dialect.

It is highly probable that the causes of their disappearance are manifold. There is frequently to be observed in certain speech-levels, and especially in English, with its love of understatement, an attempt to avoid terms that are thought of as unpleasant or too vehement and to replace them by more euphemistic expressions. The *NED* makes note of this in connection with the substantive *lie.*[21] Such a tendency may have operated in a general way to weaken the position of *lease* 'falsehood' and related words in the language. More special influences may also have been at work. The adjective *lease* 'false, untrue' first became obsolete. But it became obsolete only in this sense. OE *lēas* meant also 'without, free from, devoid of' and in these senses has come into Modern English, not as an independent word except in dialect, but as the suffix -*less,* "which was, and still is, very freely attached to sbs. to form adjs. with privative sense."[22] This use of the OE word may have predominated even to the point of weakening the word in its other senses. Probably still other influences were operating to force these words out of the standard language. If homonymy and consequent confusion with other words were among such influences—and Hemken's point is a reasonable one—it is to be found as he has suggested in connection with the substantive. The verb *lease* 'to tell lies' was homonymous with *lease* 'to glean, gather,' from OE *lesan* (later to be considered somewhat more fully), but confusion between them was not likely. Middle English *lease* 'to tell lies' was pronounced [lɛːzə], as the 16th-century spelling indicates, and so did not fall together in sound with the verb *lease* [lɛːs], from Anglo-French *lesser;* the related noun *leasing* 'falsehood, lying' preserves the form with [z] today in the dialects of Scotland and the North of England.

In the case of the substantives, however, confusion was more

21. *NED, Lie* sb.[1]: "In mod. use, the word is normally a violent expression of moral reprobation, which in polite conversation tends to be avoided, the synonyms *falsehood* and *untruth* being often substituted as relatively euphemistic."

22. See *NED,* under -*less.*

probable. The Anglo-French word *les* was a legal term used in England as early as the 13th century and must have been introduced about 1100, as is indicated by its Norman, as opposed to Central, French form. By the 16th century it had become a commonly used, fully naturalized English word. It had from the beginning its present meanings: 'a contract between parties, by which property is transferred from one to another for a period of time, etc.' With its long history as a legal term taken over from French into the English law-court parlance behind it, it would hold a secure place in English once it became a common term. This *lease* was pronounced in Middle English [lɛ:s]: OF *lais, leis,* AF *les* became ME *lese,* with open *ẹ̄* before the dental, as in *peace,*[23] and with final voiceless -[s].

With this word OE *lēas* 'falsehood' developed phonetic identity; *lēas* became ME *lẹ̄s* [lɛ:s], spelled *lease, lesse, leace,* etc., with the same open *ẹ̄*-sound and final voiceless -[s]. When words with exactly the some sound meant both 'a legal contract' and 'a lie, an untruth,' ambiguity was sure to arise if both were kept in ordinary speech. Even by early Middle English times the native word was, to a great extent, restricted to its adjectival use and to certain phrases like *but lease, without(en lease.* But by the end of the 16th century, after *lease* 'a contract' had become a common word, it was obsolete. And the loss of the substantive may have hastened the loss of the verb.

In one form, however, the substantive survived, a form differentiated from the French derivative. OE *lēasung* became ME *leasing* 'a lie, a falsehood, lying.' This word continued in use into the 18th century and is today to be found in dialectal speech in Scotland, Northumberland, and Yorkshire.[24]

iii. Heal *and* Hele[25]

There were in Old English two related verbs both meaning 'to hide, to conceal, to keep secret,' *helan* and a later form *helian* (for older *hellan*). *Helan* was a strong verb of the ablaut series *hel-, hal-, hul-,* cognate with OHG *helan,* MnG *hehlen.* OE *helian* was a weak verb, derived ultimately from the ablaut-grade *hal-,* Gmc. **haljan.* Both *helan* and *helian* appear in Middle English as *hele* (cf. *NED, Hele* v.[1] and v.[2]), recognizable in the strong and weak forms, respectively, of tenses other than the present. In the present tense the two coincided. Gradually they coalesced throughout, the strong forms of *helan* disappearing from use in the course of the 14th century. The

23. Jordan, *Handbuch,* § 233.   24. Wright, *EDD.*
25. These words are discussed in this connection by Menner, "The Conflict of Homonyms in English," pp. 234–5. They are also mentioned, far more summarily, by Offe, *Das Aussterben alter Verba,* p. 25. They are included here for the sake of completeness, since they offer a striking instance of conflict which arose in consequence of the sound-changes under discussion.

verb with the meaning 'to cover, to conceal' was, then, *hēle* [hɛːlə] with long open *ē* after the lengthening of OE *e* in open syllables, in the early 13th century.

But another native English verb had been, for about a century, pronounced with exactly this sound. OE *hǣlan* 'to cure, to make whole,' derived from Gmc. **hailo-z,* adj., had in its accented syllable the *ǣ* that was common Old English (exc. Kent.) (Jordan, § 48). OE *ǣ* became ME *ē* in the 12th century, and *hǣlan* thus became *hēle* [hɛːlə] in all of England except Kent.

When, therefore, OE *helan* became *hēle* in the course of the following century, the two verbs were identical in sound. They were, in addition, antagonistic in sense; *to hēle a wound, a cut, a sore* was either 'to cure it' or 'to cover, to conceal it.' Barbour's "Snaw had helit all the land"[26] might be understood as a figurative use of the verb *hele* 'to cure, heal' rather than an example (as it is) of *hele* 'to cover.'

The two verbs existed side by side for some time. *Hele, heal* 'to cure, to make whole' was one of a wide family of words, many of which had been in the language from Old English times: *healer* 'one who heals'; *healing* 'curing, cure; curative'; *heal*, sb. 'health'; *health* 'soundness of body'; *healness* 'welfare, salvation'; *healless* 'deprived of health'; *healsome* 'healthful'; *healend* 'one that saves, the Saviour'; etc. *Hele* 'to hide, to cover' was less firmly supported by derivative and related words, though it was not without them: *heling* 'a covering'; *hele*, sb. 'concealment'; *heler* 'one who covers up or conceals.' Both verbs had synonyms—*to heal, to cure; to hele, to cover, to hide, to conceal, to keep secret.* Perhaps this very richness of choice among verbs meaning 'to cover' led speakers and writers of English to abandon more and more the ambiguous *to hele.* And one suspects also that the ambiguity between the two was felt, that it operated actively against the word *hele* 'to cover' very soon after homonymy developed, for it was in the 14th century that the synonyms from French began to appear commonly in English records: *to cover*, an adaptation of OF *cuvrir, covrir*, appears in 13th-century documents, but became frequent in the sense 'to put or lay something over (an object) with the effect of hiding from view' only in the 14th century; *to conceal*, adaptation of OF *conceler*, is first recorded in 1375, according to data in the *NED; secret*, in *to keep secret*, came into use in the late 14th century.

Hele 'to hide, to cover,' by the end of the 16th century, or earlier, had become archaic in Standard English, as the 1625 quotation in the *NED* indicates quite clearly: "In this Countrie, with them that retaine the ancient language . . . to hell the dead, is as much as to cover the dead."[27] But, though it was archaic in Standard English,

---

26. *NED*, see *Hele* v.² 2. 'to cover.'   27. Ussher, *Answ. Jesuit*, 287.

the word continued in use as a dialectal word and is still so used in various parts of England, Scotland, and Ireland, "esp[ecially]," says the *NED*, "in senses (a) to cover (roots, seeds, etc.) with earth; (b) to cover with slates or tiles, to roof." Wright's records show it in wide use in various senses—'to hide, conceal; to keep secret; to cover; to wrap up, to tuck up the bedclothes, etc.' In the sense 'to cover' it is in use in the United States: "Just heel those roses in; I'll set them properly next spring." It is always construed with *in*—*to heel in.*[28]

There is evidence that ME *ẹ̄* from OE *e* in open syllables and ME *ę̄* from OE *ǣ* (from WGmc. *ai*) do not coincide in all dialects, as they do in Standard English,[29] that in southwest Yorkshire, south, mid-south and southwest Lancashire, Northamptonshire, Cheshire, Derbyshire, Leicestershire, Herefordshire, and Dorset they are kept apart. Particular dialect studies, to some extent, bear out the differentiation of the two. In the dialect of Huddersfield, in southwest Yorkshire, for example, *iel* [iəl] means 'to heal,' *ill, ull* [il, ul] mean 'to cover up.'[30] But data are not yet specific or detailed enough to reveal clearly the status of the two words generally in dialect, though we may suspect that this differentiation of the two sounds played some part in preserving *hele, heal* 'to cover.'

In German, we note, where the two did not become homonyms, both survive—*heilen* 'to heal' and *hehlen* 'to conceal.'

iv. Breed *and* Brede

J. Offe, in his study of homonyms in English, gives the following instance:

ā·brǣdan > *brēden* „braten" ist infolge lautgesetzlicher Entwicklung angl. u. kent. nicht mehr zu unterscheiden von me. *brēden* < *brēdan* ne. to breed „brüten," seine Bedeutung geht auf *rosten* > *to roast* über, während für *brǣdan* „breit machen" die Neubildung *to broaden* eintritt.[31]

Offe's instance is a good one, with more points of interest than his very brief comment indicates. OE (Angl.) *brēdan* (Sax. *brǣdan*) 'to roast' and OE *brēdan* 'to breed' became full homonyms in Middle English:

Gmc. *brǣð-an* became OE (Angl.) *brēdan*, ME *brẹ̄de*.
Gmc. *brōðjan* became OE *brēdan*, ME *brẹ̄de*.
Confusion was, in this case, inevitable, when *to breed geese, pigs,*

28. Cf. *Dictionary of American English on Historical Principles.*
29. Wright, *Elementary Middle English Grammar*, § 52, Note 1: "Although the two sounds have fallen together in standard NE. they are still kept apart in many of the north Midland dialects, the former having became *iə* and the latter *ei*. . . ." See also data in Wright, *EDGr.*
30. Haigh, *A New Glossary of the Dialect of the Huddersfield District.*
31. Offe, *Das Aussterben alter Verba*, p. 22.

chickens meant both 'to roast' them and 'to raise' them. Such confusion must have arisen early; by 1297 *to roast,* the substitute term for *to brede,* begins to appear in records. By 1500 *brede* 'to roast' was obsolete.

It had, perhaps, the chance of surviving in Saxon areas, where the root vowel was not the close *ẹ̄* of the Anglian forms and of the homonym *brede* 'to breed,' but open *ẹ̄.* But in this case the substantive *brẹ̄d(e* 'roast meat' [brɛːd(ə] would have met opposition from the substantive *bread, brẹ̄d* [brɛːd], from OE *brēad* 'bread.'[32] In both Anglian and Saxon areas the verb or its related substantive was homonymous with a word with which confusion was not only probable but unavoidable. *Brede,* sb. 'roast meat' became obsolete after *c*1420 (16th-century quot. doubtful), except for a possible survival in the compound form *sweetbread* and the Scottish dialectal form, occurring always in the plural, *breeds, brids* [briːdz, bridz] 'the pancreas, esp. of sheep, i.e., the sweetbread.'[33] *Brede,* v. 'to roast,' says the *NED,* "passed entirely out of use *c*1500."

In German, where homonymy did not develop, all three terms survive:

Verb	OHG *bruotan* 'to breed'	*brātan* 'to roast'	
	MHG *brüeten*	*brāten*	
	MnG *brüten*	*braten*	
Sb.	OHG *brāto* 'roast meat'	*brōt* 'bread'	
	MnG *der Braten*	*Brod, Brot*	

v. Bread *and Its Homonyms*

The possibilities of confusion and interference between the word *bread* and its homophones are more numerous than the circumstances mentioned in the preceding section indicate, and one is tempted to ask if the immediate impetus to its irregular sound-development, even in view of the fact that the same irregularity was shared by a number of other words similarly constructed phonetically, might not have been homonymic interference. Why is Modern English *bread* pronounced [brɛd], and not [briːd] as might have been expected?

Luick shows (*Hist. Gram.,* § 525) that the shortening of *ẹ̄* to [ɛ], occurring in the 15th and 16th centuries, was shared by a group of words of one syllable ending in a consonant—*bread, dead, head, lead,* sb., etc.—while it did not occur in the case of others, e.g., *lead,* v., *read, mead, plead,* etc.

OE *brēad* 'bread' became ME *brẹ̄d,* being pronounced [brɛːd] during the whole ME period. As shown above, OE *brǣde* 'roast meat' also became ME *brẹ̄d(e* [brɛːd(ə]. A third word, OE *brǣd* 'a trick,

32. See the following section.   33. Grant, *The Scottish National Dictionary.*

a twist' also became ME *brēd* [brɛ:d], though this form of the word was of less frequent occurrence than the variant form *breid(e, braid* (from OE *brægd*); the word was commonly used in this sense in Middle English and early Modern English times, and from 1530 on in the sense 'plait (of hair).' Still a fourth word, OE *brǣd, brǣdu* 'breadth, width' became ME *brēd(e* [brɛ:d(ə]. All four substantives would have become, by normal phonological development, Modern English [bri:d]; only one of the four exists today with that pronunciation.

Confusion between *brēd* 'bread' and *brēd* 'roast meat' almost certainly led to the loss of the latter. *Brēd* 'bread' remained in use. But *brēd* meant also 'trick' and 'plait (of hair)' and 'width, breadth.' It seems very likely that there would be interference between these various words. At just about the time, that is, in the early 16th century, that *brēd* 'trick, twist' took the meaning 'plait (of hair)' and began to be frequently used in that sense in both its variant forms *brēd* and *braid*, *brēd* 'bread' took the pronunciation [brɛd], with shortened vowel before the final dental, and *brēd* 'width, breadth' began to be replaced by the late analogical formation *breadth* (1523 on). The older form *brede* 'breadth' is found in modern dialects of Scotland and the North of England, with the pronunciation [bri:d]. Thus only one of the four substantives continued along normal lines of development: *brēd* 'bread' is [brɛd], not [bri:d]; *brēd* 'roast meat' is obsolete; *brēd* 'plait' yielded place entirely to its variant *braid* [breid]; *brēde* 'width' was replaced by *breadth*, with shortened vowel and distinguishing suffix, except in a limited area in dialect, where it has the form *bread, brede, breid,* etc., [bri:d]. It seems more than likely that homonymic interference played an active part in the development of this group of words.

IV

Conflict of Queen *and* Quean

IN the late 17th or early 18th century ME *ę̄* became MnE [iː],[1] and thus coincided with ME *ẹ̄*, which had reached the grade [iː] in the 15th century.[2] ME *hę̄le* [hɛːlə] became, for example, MnE [hiːl], spelled *heal*. Many words were involved in this change, and many new sets of homonyms were produced. The words *queen* and *quean* were among them;[3] their history prior to and subsequent to this period offers a convincing illustration of the possible effect of homonymy on the life of words.

Both *queen* and *quean* are native English words. Both have cognates in Gothic and other Germanic languages, and can be traced to hypothetical Germanic and Indo-European forms ultimately related by ablaut:

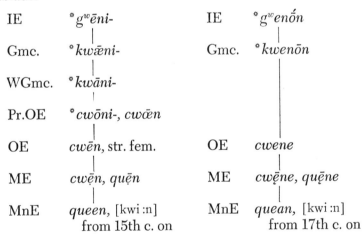

IE	*$g^w\bar{e}ni$-	IE	*$g^w en\acute{o}n$
Gmc.	*$kw\bar{æ}ni$-	Gmc.	*$kwen\bar{o}n$
WGmc.	*$kw\bar{a}ni$-		
Pr.OE	*$cw\bar{o}ni$-, *cwǣn*		
OE	*cwēn*, str. fem.	OE	*cwene*
ME	*cwę̄n*, *quę̄n*	ME	*cwę̄ne*, *quę̄ne*
MnE	*queen*, [kwiːn]	MnE	*quean*, [kwiːn]
	from 15th c. on		from 17th c. on

Gothic *qēns*, ON *kvān*, OS *quân* correspond to OE *cwēn*; Gothic *qinō*, OS *quena*, OHG *quina*, *quena*, ON *kvenna*, *kvinna* correspond to OE *cwene*.

Queen, even in Old English times, had its present meaning, 'the wife or consort of a king,' from which figurative uses developed, as, for example, 'the chief or most beautiful thing of its class.' It was not used, or very seldom used, to mean 'wife' or 'woman' in the ordinary sense.

1. Luick, *Hist. Gram.*, § 499.
2. *Ibid.*, §§ 479 ff. Early periods in the history of these two sounds also offer, as has been shown, instances of homonymic confusion.
3. Menner, "Conflict of Homonyms in English," pp. 232–3.

Cwene, from which *quean* developed, meant in Old English 'woman' but early in Middle English times took on a derogatory sense, 'a bold woman,' 'a harlot.'

The two words were kept distinct phonetically throughout Middle English times. *Cwēn* 'queen' had the close *ẹ̄* that became [iː] in the 15th century; *cwene* had the open *ẹ̄* that was maintained throughout Middle English times and only in the late 17th or early 18th century finally reached the grade [iː], spelled here, as in many words of the same class, *ea.* They were, then, clearly differentiated phonetically through a long period of their history, and, therefore, were not likely to collide. But when, finally, with the change of *ẹ̄* [ɛː] into [iː], they did become identical in sound, it was only to be expected that confusion and resulting conflict should arise between them. Speakers would not easily tolerate the same group of phonemes as the designation for the wife of the king, or the sovereign herself, and for a common woman, a woman of the streets.

Quean is now an archaic or obsolescent word in Standard English.[4] This gradual disuse and loss of the term is an indication of the process by which a language avoids situations of the kind. *Queen* was always the more firmly established word in the standard language, and when conflict arose maintained its place and thus forced the less used word into obsolescence.

But the evidence from Standard English, though clear, is not sufficient basis for conclusive deductions. Words meaning 'harlot, strumpet' tend naturally to disappear from so-called "polite" language, both spoken and written. It can be pointed out, also, that *quean* 'an ill-behaved woman, a harlot' is used by writers with far less frequency than is *queen* even before the time at which the two became homonyms. *Quean* appears in Chaucer's works only twice,[5] in Shakespeare's three or four times,[6] in Spenser's once,[7] in Marlowe's once,[8] in Thomas Kyd's twice.[9] In every case *queen* is a very frequently used word. *Quean* probably never had the firm status as a literary word that *queen* held. It was, nevertheless, a living term in

4. So marked in Wyld's *Universal Dictionary of the English Language.*

5. See J. S. P. Tatlock and A. G. Kennedy, *A Concordance to the Complete Works of Geoffrey Chaucer and to the Romaunt of the Rose,* Carnegie Institution of Washington, 1927.

6. See John Bartlett, *A New and Complete Concordance or Verbal Index to Words, Phrases, & Passages in the Dramatic Works of Shakespeare,* London, 1913.

7. See C. G. Osgood, *A Concordance to the Poems of Edmund Spenser,* Carnegie Institution of Washington, Publ. No. 189, 1915.

8. See C. Crawford, *The Marlowe Concordance* (Part VI), *Materials for the Study of the Old English Drama,* being the completion and continuation of the *Materialien zur Kunde des älteren Englischen Dramas,* New Series, Vol. VI, Louvain, 1931.

9. See C. Crawford, *A Concordance to the Works of Thomas Kyd, Materialien zur Kunde des älteren Englischen Dramas,* XV, Louvain, 1906.

the language, even in the standard language, until the fact of homonymy served to weaken its hold and finally to dislodge it.[10]

That homonymy with the more strongly entrenched word did serve
to undermine the position of *quean* is more clearly evidenced by
dialects. *Quean* is still a living term in several sections of England,
and the circumstances of its existence in dialect are of special significance for the present study.

Wright lists *quean* as a word in ordinary dialectal use in Scotland,
Northumberland, Durham, Cumberland, Yorkshire, Lancashire, and
in Wiltshire, Somerset, and Devon—two distinct areas, one Northern
and North Midland, the other Southwestern. (See Map 3, p. 91, and
Note below.) It is used in these areas to mean 'a woman, a damsel,' as a
term of endearment for a little girl, in combinations such as *quean-
bairn* 'a female child,' and, to quote, as "a term of reproach for a
shrewish or dirty woman," 'an immoral woman.' In particular localities the connection varies; in Scotland, Jamieson tells us, the word

is never meant as implying any reproach, unless an epithet, conveying
this idea, be conjoined with it. Although familiar, it is often used as ex-
pressive of kindness. . . . It is never a respectful designation; but it is
often used, in familiar language, without any intentional disre-
spect. . . .[11]

In the North Riding of Yorkshire, also, and in the dialect of Cleveland the word, here appearing in the form *weean*, etc., carries no dis-
respect.[12] But very frequently it does carry this connotation, as it
does in Standard English. In either case, though more particularly
when it has the derogatory significance, there would be conflict between this term and *queen* as the designation for the ruler of the
land or the wife of the ruler and as a word used figuratively to mean
'the finest of its class.'

There would be conflict, that is, so long as the two words remained identical in sound. But evidence of two kinds shows that
they are quite generally differentiated in sound, through normal

10. In contrast to this steady use of the term by early writers, limited though it is,
is its almost total absence from writings after the early 18th century. Compare, for
example, concordances to the works of Pope, Keats, Shelley, Wordsworth, in which
quean does not appear at all. Browning uses it once. Such a comparison, though not
in any way conclusive, emphasizes the fact that *quean* is now an obsolescent term.

Note on Map 3:
Luick's phonetic symbols appear in legend of Map 3. Read, as explanation of dotted
line: "Area where ẹ̄ and ẹ̆ remain distinct as [e:] and [i:] respectively." Read, as explanation of solid line: "Area where ẹ̄ and ẹ̆ remain distinct as [iə] and [i:], or as [i:]
and [ei] respectively."

11. Jamieson, *Etymological Dictionary of the Scottish Language*, under *Queine,
quean, queyn.*

12. Pease, *Dictionary of the Dialect of the North Riding of Yorkshire;* J. C. Atkinson, *A Glossary of the Cleveland Dialect*, London, 1868.

dialectal developments, in those areas where *quean* persists as a living term.

The first kind of evidence is that presented by Luick in his studies of the development of ME $\bar{e}$ and $\bar{e}$.[13] This is general and must be supplemented by special dialect studies, the second kind of evidence, in which the two words are specifically considered.

ME $\bar{e}$ [e:] became general English [i:] in the 15th century,[14] with a few minor variations to be mentioned later. Thus OE *cwēn* [kwe:n] 'queen' became *queen* [kwi:n] in most of England and Scotland.

ME $\bar{e}$, on the other hand, had, in dialects, a varied development, its history being closely linked with that of ME $\bar{a}$.[15] In most of the Midlands and in the Southeast it reached the grade [i:] in the late 17th or early 18th century, thus falling together with ME $\bar{e}$. It is to be noted that *quean* does not appear in the dialects of these sections.

But in those very areas where *quean* does appear in dialect there is to be observed a tendency toward differentiation of the two sounds, a tendency that may well account, at least in part, for the persistence of the word there. In the Southwest, for example, within an area embracing Cornwall, Devon, Somerset, part of Dorset, Gloucester, Worcester, south Warwick, southwest Northampton, and Oxford (see Map 3), ME $\bar{e}$ has remained as [e:]. Thus ME $\bar{e}$ and ME $\bar{e}$ are kept distinct, $\bar{e}$ having there become [i:]. This area includes that in which *quean* is found, with the exception of Wiltshire (see Map 3). But the example from Wiltshire is a doubtful one. It is recorded, say the editors of the *Wiltshire Glossary*,[16] as a word "not as yet . . . met with by ourselves in this county, although given by some authority or other as used in Wilts." It appears, moreover, in the northwest of the county, Castle Eaton, and is thus very close to the area in which Luick shows that the two vowel-sounds were kept apart.

In the northern and western Midlands, also, and in parts of the North, ME $\bar{e}$ and ME $\bar{e}$ are kept distinct as [iə] and [i:] or as [i:] and [ei] respectively.[17] Yorkshire, Westmorland, and Cumberland are included in this, and parts of Lancashire, Derby, Northumberland, and south Cheshire, with other scattered points[18] (see Map 3). Reference to the map will show the striking coincidence of these areas with those in which *quean* appears as a living dialectal word.[19]

13. Luick, *Hist. Gram.*, §§ 497 ff., 479 ff.; and *Untersuchungen zur englischen Lautgeschichte* (Strassburg, 1896), §§ 145 ff.

14. Luick, *Hist. Gram.*, § 479, § 480.   15. *Ibid.*, §§ 492 ff. and 497 ff.

16. G. E. Dartnell and E. H. Goddard, *A Glossary of Words Used in the County of Wiltshire*, English Dialect Society, Series C, Original Glossaries, No. 69, London, 1893. See *quean* and explanation of symbols preceding text.

17. Luick, *Hist. Gram.*, § 497, especially Note 5. Luick's phonetic symbols are here changed into the corresponding IPA.

18. See Luick, *Untersuchungen*, § 195, § 199.

19. Its persistence in Scotland, in Durham, and in parts of Northumberland, however, cannot thus be accounted for.

Special dialect studies are as yet not sufficiently detailed or numerous to offer convincing support at this point. The words do not appear in Haigh's study of the dialect of Huddersfield. In J. Wright's *Grammar of the Dialect of Windhill, in the West Riding of Yorkshire*, *queen* [kwiːn] 'queen' appears, but not *quean;* studies of the vowel-sounds involved, however, given in the earlier sections of the book, indicate their differentiation in this dialect.[20] The spelling of *Queen Anners* 'old-fashioned tales' and *queean* 'a slut, a harlot' in F. K. Robinson's *Glossary of Words Used in the Neighbourhood of Whitby*[21] may indicate a different pronunciation in that locality.

But such special studies offer more abundant evidence of another kind of differentiation between the two words *queen* and *quean,* one that seems, like the former, to be part of normal dialectal trends.

There is, in the Northern and North Midland counties, a marked tendency for words in *qu-* to appear with initial *w-* or *wh-*. Wright's records and various dialect studies show this. It is to be observed in connection with such words as *cushion, quake, quaker, quaint, queem* 'pleasant,' *querken* 'to choke,' *quick* 'alive,' *quicken* 'mountain ash,' *quiet, quite* 'to requite,' which appear as *wishin, whake, whaker, waint* (*whaint*), *wheem, whirken, whick* (*wick, whik*), *hwicken* (*wicken*), etc. respectively.[22] The variation is frequent in Scotland, Cumberland, Northumberland, Durham, Westmorland, Lancashire, Yorkshire, Cheshire, Derby (see Map 4, p. 93), and occurs occasionally in the other Midland counties and even in the extreme South and Southwest.[23]

The word *quean* shares this tendency; it is found with great frequency in the forms *wean, whean,* etc. Wright lists the forms *wean, weean, whean, wheen, whein* as occurring in north, northeast, middle, west, and east Yorkshire, in Lancashire, in Durham, in two collections of North Country words, and in north Devon (see Map 4).[24] In the North Riding of Yorkshire *weean* means 'a woman, a wife,' and *weeanish* 'womanly; effeminate, if used of males.'[25] In the section of country around Whitby are to be heard *weean* 'a quean, wench, woman,' *weean-cat* 'a she-cat,' *weean-craft, weean-craz'd, weean-fond, weean-hefted, weean-house, weeanish, weean-*

20. J. Wright, *A Grammar of the Dialect of Windhill, in the West Riding of Yorkshire*, English Dialect Society, Series C, Original Glossaries, No. 67 (London, 1892), §§ 87 and 147, 39 and 43.

21. F. K. Robinson, *A Glossary of Words Used in the Neighbourhood of Whitby* (Part 2), English Dialect Society, Series C, Original Glossaries, Part IV, London, 1876.

22. Wright, *English Dialect Grammar*, § 241 and Index.

23. Wright states, for example, that *hw, w* occur in *quicken* 'mountain ash' in Devon (as well as in the North), in *quilkin* 'a toad' in Cornwall, and that *squeamish* has *sw-* in Dorset and Somerset and in the North. See *English Dialect Grammar*, § 241.

24. Wright, *EDD*, under *Quean*.

25. Pease, *A Dictionary of the Dialect of the North Riding of Yorkshire*.

strucken.[26] In the Cleveland dialect occur *weean* 'a female, a woman, a wife'; *weeanish, weean-strucken.*[27] Morris's dictionary of the Yorkshire dialect gives *wean* 'a female' and states that it is used for the most part in a bad sense.[28] Other works might be cited to the same effect.

This phonetic differentiation through the initial consonants must have been a factor in the preservation of the word in these particular areas, just as differentiation through the vowel-sound was.

Material is not available for a detailed study of the probable reasons for its survival in Scotland, but in general the vowel sounds concerned have taken there a differing course of development. In a large part of that country ME $\bar{e}$ and ME $\bar{ẹ}$ normally remained distinct: in southeast Scotland the two sounds fell together as [iː], but elsewhere ME $\bar{ẹ}$ became [iː] and $\bar{ẹ}$ fell together in sound with ME $\bar{a}$ [ɑː] and shared its developments.[29] William Grant's *Scottish National Dictionary* indicates particular areas in which OE *e* in open syllables took, in Modern Scots, a sound differing from that into which OE $\bar{ẹ}$ developed, the latter becoming [iː] "as generally also in Eng.—e.g. . . . deed, sleep . . . teeth,"[30] the former being "lengthened and [taking] the sound of *a* in *mate* [ei] in some dialects, and *ee* [iː] in others."[31] Jamieson lists *queen* (in *queen's-cake* 'a white sweet cake' and *queen's cushion* 'a plant' and 'a mode of carriage') and *queine, quean, queyn* 'a young woman.'[32] Future dialect studies of specific areas may throw further light on this particular question in Scotland.

The history of the words in England and, so far as it can be studied, in Scotland supports the theory of homonymic conflict as a cause of the loss of one of them. Since homonymy developed, *quean* has steadily lost ground in the standard literary language and disappeared as a spoken word. It is, indeed, not a familiar word to people

26. Robinson, *A Glossary of Words Used in the Neighbourhood of Whitby.*
27. Atkinson, *A Glossary of the Cleveland Dialect.*
28. Morris, *Yorkshire Folk-Talk.*
29. Luick, *Hist. Gram.,* § 497.2.
30. W. Grant, *The Scottish National Dictionary,* Vol. I, Part 1, Introd. § 41.
31. *Ibid.,* § 57 (The phonetic symbols of the IPA have here and in the rest of this note been substituted for Grant's). Later, in § 88, he states that OE *e* in open position takes the [ei] as in *fate* in East Mid Scots in a district north of the Forth, but [iː] in the section of the East Mid Scots south of the Forth, [iː] in West Mid Scots (§ 93.3), and in South Mid Scots (§ 96.2). In Southern Scots and again in much of Northern Scots, OE open *e* has developed into sounds differentiated distinctly from that of OE $\bar{ẹ}$. See §§ 104, 121, 126.2 where the word *quean* is listed. Grant's and Luick's data agree, as study of the above and of Grant's map (opp. p. xxv) quickly reveals.
Data in Grant's *Dictionary,* though limited as yet, bear out in an interesting way the fact of differentiation of the two sounds. See pronunciations given for *beet* 'to mend, repair' (< OE *bētan*), and for *bear* (< OE *beran*) and *beat* with ME $\bar{ẹ}$ from OE *ēa* in *bēatan.*
32. *Wean, weeane* are given, but mean 'a child' (possibly *wee ane*). *Wheen* means 'queen' in Shetland but is not listed for Scotland.

who are not readers of older literature. In dialects it does not appear in areas where the vowel-sounds involved became identical. It does, on the other hand, survive in dialects as a living term in areas where differentiation is made probable through two distinct trends—developments in the vowel-sounds which preserved their differentiation and a development of the initial consonant which, apparently, affected one word and not the other. Special dialect studies, though incomplete, frequently show that when the two exist together it is as forms differing phonetically, between which confusion and conflict were not possible.

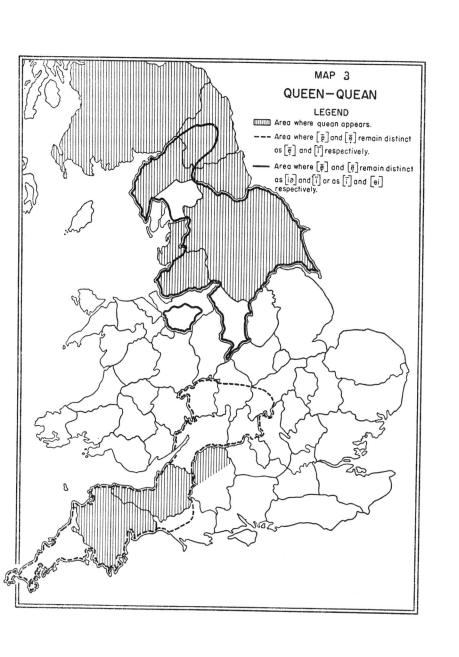

MAP 3

QUEEN—QUEAN

LEGEND

▥ Area where quean appears.

--- Area where [ē̜] and [ē̜] remain distinct as [ē̜] and [ī] respectively.

— Area where [ē̜] and [ē̜] remain distinct as [iə] and [ī] or as [ī] and [ei] respectively.

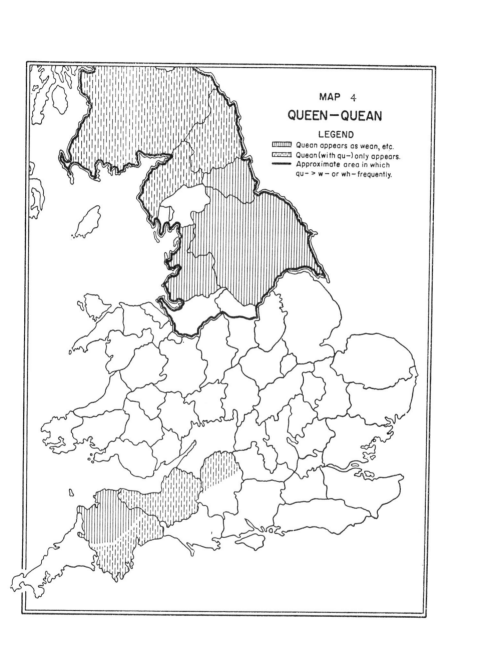

MAP 4

QUEEN—QUEAN

LEGEND

Quean appears as wean, etc.
Quean (with qu-) only appears.
Approximate area in which
qu- > w- or wh- frequently.

V

Conflicts Involving ME ai

A SERIES of sound-changes, most of them involving the vo-
calization of OE ʒ, culminated, in the second half of the 13th
century or earlier, in the Middle English diphthong *ai.*

a) OE æ + ʒ had, in OE, become *æi,* and this with the change of
æ into *a,* which took place from 1100 on, became *ai* (Jordan,
§ 93. Jespersen, § 3.611).[1]

b) OE ǣ + ʒ became late OE *ẹ̄i,* and about 1200 was shortened to
ẹi. As in the following case, *ẹi* became *ai* in the second half of
the 13th century (Jordan, § 94. Jespersen, § 3.613).

c) OE e + ʒ became *ẹi* in the 12th century, then *æi,* then *ai* in the
second half of the 13th century (Jordan, § 95. Jespersen,
§ 3.612).

d) OE ē + ʒ, at the end of word or syllable, became *ẹ̄i* in late OE.
This sound was shortened and changed to *ẹi* in time to share
the change into *ai* (Jordan, § 97).

e) ON *æi, ei,* West Norse *ey* fell together with English *ei* and with
it became *ai* in the second half of the 13th century (Jordan,
§ 130).

f) OF *ai,* at the end of words, and before a vowel, before liquids,
before nasals, was kept in ME (Jordan, § 233. Jespersen,
§ 3.615).

g) OF (Norm.) *ei,* under certain conditions, became ME *ai* (Jordan, § 234. Jespersen, § 3.616).

The consequence was that in Middle English, from the late 13th century on, a diphthong existed which could be traced to these various
sources and to others not given here.[2] They may be graphically represented thus:

		12th c.	Early 13th c.	Late 13th c.
OE æʒ > æi >	ME	*ai*		
OE ǣʒ > ẹ̄i >			*ẹi* >	*ai*
OE eʒ >		*ẹi* >	*æi* >	*ai*
OE ēʒ > ẹ̄i >			*ẹi* >	*ai*
ON *æi, ei, ey* >		*ei*	>	*ai*
OF *ai* >		*ai* (under certain conditions)		
OF *ei* >		*ai* (under certain conditions)		

1. The references to Jespersen in this section are to *A Modern English Grammar on
Historical Principles* (3d ed., Heidelberg, 1931), Part 1 on Sounds and Spelling.
References to Jordan are to the *Handbuch.*

2. For example, Wright shows in § 107.4 of the *EMEGr.* that late OE *e* (early
WS *ea*) + *h* or *ht* became early ME *ei* (*ey*), then *ai* (*ay*) about 1300. See also
Jordan, *Handbuch*, § 96, where the date of the change of the *ei* of this origin into
ai is given as the 15th century.

Such a series of changes produced many new homonyms in the language and thus opened the way for possible confusion between words heretofore independent of one another. Such was the case between OE *weӡan* 'to bear, carry; to weigh,' OE *wǣӡan* 'to trouble, afflict; to deceive,' and in certain forms, later to be mentioned in detail, OE *wecgan* 'to shake, toss'; between OE *treӡian* 'to trouble, to grieve' and the ME derivative of OF *traïr* 'to betray'; between OE *fæӡnian* 'to rejoice' and ME *feinen*, from OF *feindre* (present participle *feignant*) 'to pretend'; and between OE *swēӡan* 'to make a noise, roar,' OE *swīӡan* 'to be silent,' and the ME verb *sweӡe*, late 15th-century *sway* of uncertain history.

i. Conflict of Weigh
and its Homonyms

OE *weӡan* was a strong verb, with cognates in all branches of the Germanic language family. It was a common verb in Middle English, used in various connections with the general meanings 1) 'to bear, carry, hold up; to heave up, lift,' now more or less restricted to the nautical expressions *to weigh anchor*, etc.; 2) 'to balance in the scales'; and 3) 'to have heaviness or weight.' It occurred in several Middle English forms: *weiӡe, weӡe* (which became *weigh*); *weie, wey; waie, waye*. The *eӡ* of the OE verb became the diphthong *ei*, which in the 13th century became *ai*, hence *weӡan* > *wei(e* > *wai(e*.

At the same time OE *ǣӡ*, through the stages *ēi* and then *ei*, became *ai* in the second half of the 13th century, OE *wǣӡan* 'to trouble, to deceive' thus becoming ME *wei(e, weye, waye*. The two were homonyms in the infinitive, in the present tense (*weӡan* in *weӡeð* forms. The *wiӡeð* forms of this verb are found only in OE), and throughout after the 13th century, when *weӡan* 'to weigh' took on the forms of the weak conjugation. Between the two verbs confusion was not very likely. OE *wǣӡan* 'to afflict' appears in ME only in the sense 'to deceive, to lead astray; to go astray'; OE *weӡan*, ME *weie, waie*, meaning 'to bear, carry, support' might conceivably be confused with it, but the 'to weigh' meanings of this verb would be sharply distinguished by context from it, and they are of frequent occurrence.

But both verbs fell together with a third in certain much-used forms. OE *wecgan* 'to move, agitate, drive hither and thither' survived into the 14th century. The third person singular of the present was *weӡeð*, and through the coincidence of this with the third person singular present *weӡeð* of the verb *weӡan* 'to move, to weigh' confusion arose between the two, apparently at an early date. The meanings of the two were particularly susceptible to confusion: *He weieð the load of hay* might mean either 'he tosses the hay' or 'he moves the hay, he weighs the hay.' The originally strong verb *weӡan*, probably in consequence of this confusion, took on forms of the weak conjugation, and the two coincided then (from the 13th century on) in past tense and past participle (*NED*, see *Weigh*, v.[1]). But *weigh* 'to shake, to toss' (*NED*, *Weigh*, v.[2]) did not survive. It was used in the 13th and even into the 14th century, but then became obsolete, its many synonyms—*to shake, to toss, to agitate*—taking its place.

In the same way the verbs *wǣӡan* (which became ME *weie, weye, waye*) 'to deceive, lead astray; to go astray' and *wecgan* 'to shake' in the third singular present and in preterite and past participial forms coincided. Confusion in use was certain; they are indeed confused in the pages of the *NED*, one and the same quotation being given to illustrate both verbs: "*c*1315 SHOREHAM, Poems I. 370 þat makeþ man so hardiliche To stonde, and so merie Ine goste, þat he ne may nauӡt yweid be Wiþ blanding ne wiþ boste." (See *NED*, *Weye*, v. and *Weigh*, v.[2]) *Weye*, from OE *wǣӡan*, is very uncommon in Middle English, and disappears entirely after the early 14th century.

Of the three verbs only *weigh*, from OE *weӡan*, is current in the English of today. The other two went out of use very shortly after homonymy developed between the three with the confusion consequent upon it.

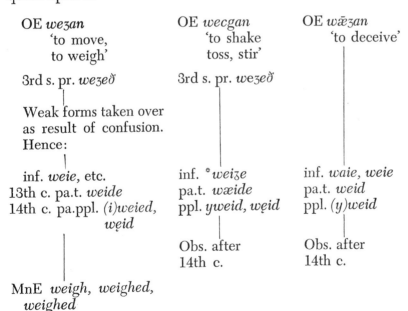

OE *weӡan*
  'to move,
  to weigh'

3rd s. pr. *weӡeð*

Weak forms taken over as result of confusion. Hence:

inf. *weie*, etc.
13th c. pa.t. *weide*
14th c. pa.ppl. *(i)weied, weid*

MnE *weigh, weighed, weighed*

OE *wecgan*
  'to shake
  toss, stir'

3rd s. pr. *weӡeð*

inf. *°weiӡe*
pa.t. *wæide*
ppl. *yweid, weid*

Obs. after 14th c.

OE *wǣӡan*
  'to deceive'

inf. *waie, weie*
pa.t. *weid*
ppl. *(y)weid*

Obs. after 14th c.

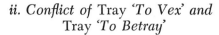

ii. Conflict of Tray *'To Vex' and*
Tray *'To Betray'*

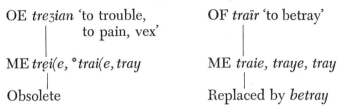

OE *treȝian* 'to trouble,   OF *traïr* 'to betray'
       to pain, vex'

ME *trẹi(e, *trai(e, tray*   ME *traie, traye, tray*

Obsolete   Replaced by *betray*

A glance at the meaning of the two Middle English verbs *tray* (*NED*, v.[1], from OE *treȝian*) and *tray* (v.[2] *ad.* OF *traïr*) shows the certainty of confusion between them. To *trẹi(e, traie one's brother* was both 'to grieve him, vex him, trouble him' and 'to betray him.' The OE verb was of longer standing in the language, but had many convenient synonyms; the French derivative was a word likely to find immediate acceptance in the French-speaking court of the 13th century and quickly succeeded in dislodging the native word, for which the several synonyms could easily be substituted. It is significant of the conflict between them that the French word itself underwent change; *to betray*, formed by the addition of English *be-* to the French adaptation, was used as early as the simple verb. And it is this form that survives. *Tray* 'to grieve, vex, trouble' became obsolete after the beginning of the 14th century, within half a century of the appearance of *tray* 'to betray.' The latter continued in use for some time, finally being replaced by *betray*.

The substantive cognate with *tray* 'to grieve, vex' was *tray* 'pain, grief, affliction, trouble.' It was used, apparently, more than two centuries longer than the verb, though for part of that time in the alliterative phrase *tray and teen, teen and tray*. It was probably in part responsible for the fact that the substantive formed in English from the French-derived verb *tray*, the substantive *tray* 'deceit, stratagem, trick,' never gained a foothold in the language. (The form *betrayal*, which has acquired a firm hold in English, is a much later formation from the corresponding verb, not appearing until the early 19th century.) Though direct confusion cannot easily arise between substantives and verbs, association through likeness in sound can be detrimental to one or both. It is perhaps significant that *tray*, v. 'to betray' and *tray*, sb. 'pain, grief' disappear finally at approximately the same time. Of the four words only *betray*, v. survives in Modern English, no trace of the others appearing even in dialect, so far as the *English Dialect Dictionary* records it.

iii. Conflict of Fain *and* Feign

Another instance of conflict between a native English word and a French borrowing is that between *fain,* v., from OE *fæʒnian* and *feine, faine, feign,* v., from OF *feindre,* pr. part. *feign-ant.* OE *fæʒnian* meant 'to rejoice'; it became ME *faine* by the end of the 13th century (see above), and was in wide use. But about 1300 a verb with the same sound came into use, *feine, faine, feigne* 'to pretend,' the Middle English form derived from the participial form *feign-ant* of the Old French verb *feindre.* OF *ei,* when it did not undergo monophthongizing before dentals, etc., as in ME *recēt,* MnE *receipt* (from ONF *receite*), remained a diphthong and fell together with *ai.*[3] The spelling *ei* was often kept, as in this case. OF *feign-ant* gave ME *feine, faine, fein* [fɛin], later [fein], MnE *feign* 'to pretend.' The construction of the two in sentences was for some time different; but when *feign* 'to pretend' began to be used with infinitive object, as it did according to the records of the *NED* early in the 15th century, such ambiguous sentences as the following were certain to confuse hearers: "They faine to praise his work," "He faines to know the truth." The native term ceased to be used generally in the 15th century; Spenser employed it much later in the *Faerie Queene,* where it was probably an archaism. The corresponding adjective *fain* continued in use, but even its support did not prevent the verb *fain* 'to rejoice' from becoming obsolete.

iv. Conflict of Sway *and Its Homonyms*

The study of these verbs involves some of the same sound changes as have the three preceding, and additional ones. It is, in some respects, a less clear case of conflict because the third verb concerned has a confused history and as yet undetermined origin, and statements as to phonetic values must in consequence be tentative. But in other respects it presents a clear instance of the part played by homonymy in the forming of the English vocabulary.

OE *swēʒan* (from *swōgjan) 'to make a noise, sound, roar' took variant forms in Middle English (see Jordan, § 97.1; Wright, *EMEGr.,* § 107.6).

When the *ēʒ* stood before a following vowel at the time of the formation of diphthongs it generally became *ei* [ei] in the North and Midlands, but *ī* [i:] . . . through the intermediate stage *īʒ* in some parts of the Midlands, especially the south Midlands including the dialect of Chaucer, and the South . . . ,

3. Jordan, *Handbuch,* § 234.

says Wright (*EMEGr.*, § 107.6). He places this change in the second half of the 13th century (*EMEGr.*, § 118); Jordan states that the [iː]-grade was reached in part in the first half of the 13th century (see § 97). Hence OE *swēʒan* became *swei(en* [swei(ən] in the North and North Midlands, and *swien* [swiː(ən] in the South Midlands and South, in the course of the 13th century. But the chief evidence for this verb in Middle English (see *NED, Swey*, v.) shows it almost exclusively in the *swei(e* forms.[4] The reason for this is to be found in the conflict that arose between it and the ME derivatives of OE *swīʒan, swīʒian* in the South Midlands and the South.

OE *swīʒan* 'to be silent' became ME *swīʒe, swīe,* by normal phonetic development, by the year 1200 (Jordan, § 90). Middle English had, in consequence, in the 13th century two verbs identical in sound, one meaning 'to make a noise, to resound,' the other 'to be silent.' Confusion was, obviously, unavoidable between them so long as both remained in the language. *Swīe* 'to be silent' became obsolete almost immediately, except possibly in one dialectal survival. *Swīe* forms of *swēʒan* 'to make a noise' vanished; *swei(e* forms survived.

But they did not survive into Modern Standard English. There was a third verb in Middle English which influenced them—*sweʒe* 'to go, move,' which appears in records for the first time in the 14th century, from an undetermined source. It had, in any case, the *eʒ* in the accented syllable that became *ei* and then *ai* from the latter half of the 13th century on, and thus coincided in sound with the *swei(e* forms of the verb meaning 'to sound, to make a noise.' Confusion between them was possible. Langland wrote: "As I lay and lenede, And loked on the watres, I slombred into a slepyng, It sweyed . . . so merrily,"[5] and meant that he nearly dozed, the water 'made such merry sounds.' But the sentence, to one hearing it as well as to one reading it, might mean also 'the water moved so merrily.' *Sweʒe* 'to go, move' is not used after 1400 except with accompanying adverb *down;* in that construction it was used more than a century longer, or until the modern *sway* 'to move to and fro,' first appearing about 1500, absorbed it. *Swey, swei(e* 'to sound' is not used after the middle of the 15th century. Both verbs went out of general use within a short time of one another.

In Wright's *English Dialect Dictionary* are given two words which may have some connection with these verbs, obsolete in Standard English since the 15th century or shortly afterward. *Swee* is given as a dialect word in Scotland and Cornwall, pronounced [swiː]. It is used as an interjection and verb, with the meaning 'to make a chirping noise.' Wright gives no reference to its origin. It may be merely

---

4. In the 14. . quotation from Langland's Prologue to *Piers Plowman* the verb appears as *sweyed,* with variant readings *swiʒede, swyed,* etc.

5. *NED,* see *Swey* v., quot. 14. . Lang.P.Pl.Prol. (ed. Wright) 10.

an onomatopoeic word; it may, on the other hand, represent the *swei(e* forms of *swēӡan* 'to make a noise,' with change in sense similar to that in the history of the word *croon*. *Swei(e*, etc., as has been stated, were Northern forms; modern dialects of the North have [iː] from older *ē* [eː] in words of this type (Wright, *EMEGr.*, § 107.6). The verb would be expected to survive in northern sections, where it was the normal development of the OE word and where confusion with *swi(e* 'to be silent' was least likely.[6] A more certain survival of OE *swēӡan* 'to sound' is found in a Scottish word listed by Wright and by Jamieson: *swech*, v. (Wright) means 'to make the sound of rushing water' as in *The swechan' lin*, quoted from the *Edinburgh Magazine* for May, 1820. From this has been formed the substantive *swechynge* 'a rushing sound as of the wind or of water falling over a precipice.' Wright refers, in connection with this word, to OE *swēgan* 'to sound, to resound.' *Swech*, sb. (Jamieson) means 'a drum.' And there is a possible trace of *swi(e* 'to be silent,' also Northern, as we should expect. *Swig* is the name, now obsolete, for a game at cards in which all the players have to remain silent, given by Wright as a North Country term, with a reference to OE *swīӡian* 'to be silent,' and by the *NED* with the same reference. The final -*g* of *swig*, however, presents difficulties if this derivation is assumed; it may have its source in Scandinavian. Such dialectal evidence, though too slight to be conclusive, may be significant.

v. Conflict of Gain, *Substantives and Verbs*

From Old Norse and Old French came into English the two substantives and the two verbs *gain—gain*, sb.[1] of the *NED*, meaning 'advantage, use, benefit,' now obsolete; *gain*, sb.[2] 'increase in possessions, etc.'; *gain*, v.[1] 'to be suitable, to avail, to meet, encounter, oppose,' now obsolete; and *gain*, v.[2] 'to obtain or secure (something which is desired or advantageous), to be benefited or advantaged, etc.'

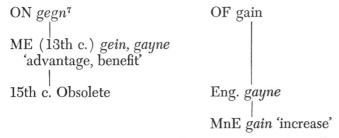

ON *gegn*[7]

ME (13th c.) *gein, gayne*
'advantage, benefit'

15th c. Obsolete

OF gain

Eng. *gayne*

MnE *gain* 'increase'

6. This does not, however, account for its appearance in Cornwall, not an originally English area.

7. The other main form of this word, ON *gagn*, gave ME *gaӡhenn*, 15th cent. Scottish *gawin*. ON *gagn* and *gegn* were "parallel forms of a sb. developed from the absol. use of the neut. of the adj. *gegn* . . ." (*NED*).

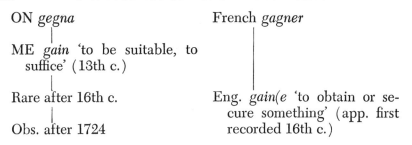

ON *gegna*   French *gagner*

ME *gain* 'to be suitable, to
   suffice' (13th c.)

Rare after 16th c.   Eng. *gain(e* 'to obtain or se-
                                       cure something' (app. first
Obs. after 1724   recorded 16th c.)

The words were homonyms. ME *-eӡ* of any origin, before the end
of the 13th century, became the diphthong *ai,* and fell together in
sound with *ai* from French *ai.*[8] The meanings of the substantives,
though distinct, were nearly allied and were certain to merge one into
the other; 'advantage, remedy' easily became 'increase in amount,
magnitude, or degree.' The verbs were somewhat more distinctly
differentiated, one being chiefly transitive, for example, *to gain ten
pounds, to gain time,* and the other intransitive, for example, *The
shoes will gain me a year* (that is, *suffice, serve me,* etc.). But they
were capable of confusion when both were used transitively or in-
transitively: *to gain opponents,* for example, meant both 'to meet
them' and 'to win them over, to persuade them.' The Old Norse
derivatives were forced out by the French borrowings, the latter,
probably, being used far more extensively and being supported by
the fashion of the day. Traces of the former were found until the
18th century in Scottish. The substantive *gain,* given by Wright as
meaning 'nearness, convenience, advantage,' may be a Yorkshire
survival from the 15th century of the substantive *gain* (from ON
gegn), but is more probably a substantive use of the adjective *gain*
(see below). It is used chiefly in the plural: "Fer gains Ah cut across
o' t' moor" (1878).[9]

The status of the adjective *gain,* from ON *gegn* 'straight, direct,
favorable, helpful,' was probably affected by the very common *gain,*
sb. and v., from French. It became obsolete in Standard English, but
survives in general dialectal use in Scotland and Northern and Midland counties (and occasionally in East Anglia, Hampshire, Somerset). It is used of a road or a direction to mean 'straight, direct'; of
things to mean 'near at hand, suitable, convenient.' It is significant
that the adjective, there being no other adjective homonymous with
it, survived to so considerable an extent, whereas the substantive and
verb from Old Norse disappeared very soon after the French importations came into use.

8. Jordan, *Handbuch,* § 190, § 93, § 95, etc.   9. Wright, *EDD, Gain* sb.[1]

vi. *Conflict of* Strait *and* Straight

Probably the most striking instance of confusion and conflict brought about by the development of *ai* in Middle English times is to be seen in the history of the two adjectives *strait* and *straight*.

Between *strait* meaning 'narrow' and *straight* meaning 'not curved, not crooked' confusion is very likely. "A strait path ran between the fields," "a straight path ran between the fields"—such sentences might occur frequently in ordinary speech, do occur, indeed, in sections of Britain where both words are still in common use; and, if the adjectives are homophones, consequent confusion is unavoidable. A *strait road*, that is, 'a narrow road'; *a strait person*, that is, 'a severe, stern person'; *a strait garment*, that is, 'a tight, close-fitting garment,' when heard only, might easily be understood to mean 'an unbending road,' 'a frank, honest person,'[10] 'a straight garment.' But the history of the two words shows again the tendency of a language to avoid such situations by changes in the form or status of one or both words.

Straight is a native term. It was originally an adjectival use of the past participle of *strecchen* 'to stretch.' This past participle, OE *streaht*,[11] became ME *streʒt*, *straʒt*, the ʒ representing the palatal sound of the OE *h* before *t*[12]: "Before *h* and *h* + consonant *ea* became *æ* (= Me. *a*, . . .) in Anglian, but *e* in late WS. . . ."[13] And from these two ME forms have developed the present forms of the word. Late OE *e* + *h* or *ht* became early ME *ei*, also written *ey*, which in most cases became *ai*, also written *ay*, about 1300.[14] Wright gives *streight* 'straight' as an example of this process: OE *streaht* became ME *streʒt*, *streight*, then *straight*. The *straucht*, *straught* forms of the word, found now in Scotland, show the later development of the Anglian *a* (from earlier *ea*, through *æ*):[15] OE *streaht* became Anglian *stræʒt*, then *straʒt*, then *straught*. The *h*, in the combination *ht*, was the palatal spirant in the *straight*, *streight* [streiχt] forms of the word; it had been lost in most of England south of the Humber by the end of the 14th century, but was kept in the North even as late as the

10. In the 16th and 17th centuries the word *straight* was used of persons to mean 'righteous, honest, frank.' Then for more than two centuries it was not so used; the present use, according to the *NED* chiefly colloquial, "is unconnected with that of the 16–17th c." See *NED*, *straight* a. 6. *Strait* 'severe, stern, strict' was used of persons from the 13th to the 17th centuries—last documented in the *NED* in 1612. Conflict between the adjectives in the two senses was, therefore, possible.

11. Cf. John R. Clark Hall, *A Concise Anglo-Saxon Dictionary*, 3d ed., Cambridge, 1931. (The 2d ed., New York, 1916, has been used also.)

12. Jordan, *Handbuch*, § 196. See also Wright, *Elementary Middle English Grammar*, § 307.

13. Wright, *Elementary Middle English Grammar*, § 28. See also Jordan, *Handbuch*, § 63.

14. Wright, *Elementary Middle English Grammar*, §§ 107 and 107.4. See also § 105.3.

15. Wright, *Elementary Middle English Grammar*, § 110.5.

19th century and in Scottish until the present time.[16] In the *straught* forms, the *h* was the ME velar [χ]; this was kept until the 15th century, but then disappeared everywhere except in Scotland and a portion of the Northwest Midlands, where it still persists.[17] The usual present-day English pronunciation [streit] differs to a marked degree, therefore, from the Scottish [strɑ:χt, streχt].

Strait 'narrow' is a French loan-word. OF *estreit* 'tight, close, narrow,' from Latin *strictus*, the past participle of *stringĕre* 'to tighten,' was adopted in Middle English in the form *streit*, with the same meanings. It appears in documents of the 13th century and became common in the 14th. OF *ei* fell together, even in Anglo-Norman, with *ai*, and in some cases, as it did in this word, remained a diphthong instead of undergoing monophthongization to *ẹ̄*. Hence *streit* became *strait*, pronounced [streit].[18] From the beginning the adjective had three chief uses, indicated by the three divisions i, ii, iii in the *NED*, as well as its use in special combinations: the physical senses, 'tight, narrow'; the uses in connection with conditions, persons, etc., 'strict, rigorous, severe'; and the senses 'limited in scope, degree, or amount.'

English had, then, the two adjectives *strait* and *straight*, particularly susceptible in most of their senses to mutual confusion. So long as the [χ] in *straight* was present in pronunciation, the two were not homonymous. But after the 14th and 15th centuries both had the same sound, and conflict between them was unavoidable.

But both did not maintain their status in English. The native word has persisted and is a common English term. The French borrowing, *strait* 'narrow,' has had a long history, but the records of the *NED* show that it has step by step lost ground. In most of its uses it is now obsolete; in some instances it is recorded as archaic, rare, or dialectal. Some thirty main and minor senses are illustrated in the *NED*: in nineteen of these it is marked *Obsolete*, in most instances since the 17th century; in four cases it is marked *Now rare*, in four *Obs. exc. dial.* (or *exc. arch.*), and in one instance *Now arch. after Bible use*. It is the influence of the Biblical passage, implied here, that has done more than anything else to maintain the adjective, so far as it is maintained, in standard literary English. The adjective occurs twice

16. See Jordan, *Handbuch*, § 295.   17. *Ibid.*, § 196, § 294.
18. While the *ei* in many words, especially when it was followed by a dental, was monophthongized to *ẹ̄*, in others the diphthong remained, e.g., *preisen* 'to praise,' *feith* 'faith.' Luick attributes this variation to the time at which the words were introduced and to influence of the "younger" Anglo-Norman form: "Je nach dem Zeitpunkt der Übernahme des Wortes oder infolge neuerlicher Beeinflussung durch die jüngere anglo-normannische Form finden sich daher im Englischen . . . für *ei* noch vorwiegend Diphthong, aber auch schon *ẹ̄*" (*Hist. Gram.*, § 416). It seems unnecessary to attribute, as Jordan does (*Handbuch*, § 234. Anm.), the persistence of the diphthong in *praise* and *strait* to the "support" of the English words *raise* and *straight*, especially in view of the fact that the [χ]-element of the latter word was still frequently pronounced when the French word was borrowed.

in the Old Testament;[19] but it is the passage in Matthew's Gospel that is most familiar to the ears of English-speaking people and that has made the word *strait* 'narrow' familiar to them:

Enter ye in at the strait gate: for wide is the gate, and broad is the way, that leadeth to destruction, and many there be which go in thereat: Because strait is the gate, and narrow is the way, which leadeth unto life, and few there be that find it.[20]

Even here the phrase has, today, been frequently interpreted, and even written, as *the straight and narrow path.* In special combinations, such as *strait-waisted,* and in special collocations, such as *strait jacket, strait work,* etc., the adjective is still in ordinary use. Outside these it has for the most part been replaced by the participial adjective *straitened,* used especially in such phrases as *in straitened circumstances, straitened means,* and by its synonyms. As adverb, also, *strait* has generally become obsolete; as substantive, with which the quasi-substantive and substantive *straight* were not easily confused, it still holds a firm place in English.

In Standard English, the adjective *strait* is undoubtedly either obsolete (in many of its senses) or archaic and rarely used (in others). In dialect this is not the case.

Straight, adjective (as well as adverb, substantive, and verb) has various dialectal uses and is found throughout England, Scotland, and Ireland. And *strait,* too, is a living dialectal word, in a more limited area. In the records of the *English Dialect Dictionary, strait* meaning 'narrow, confining; tight, hard, close; steep, etc.' is found in Scotland and in England in the counties of Durham, Yorkshire, Lancashire, Cheshire, Derbyshire, Nottinghamshire, Leicestershire, Northamptonshire, Warwickshire, Shropshire (see the maps for this study). The two words undoubtedly exist together in the living speech, in certain districts even as homonyms, as will be shown. But to a degree that is striking they are differentiated in the areas where both appear.

This is most marked in Scotland. *Strait* 'narrow' is, according to Wright, there as elsewhere pronounced [streit] and [stret]. The adjective *straight* 'unbending' appears in Scotland almost invariably in forms with [χ]: [straχt, strɑːχt, stræiχt, streχt, strɔːχt].[21] Jamieson

19. II Kings 6, 1; Isaiah 49, 20.
20. Matthew 7, 13–4, King James Version, Oxford Press. See also Luke 13, 24.
21. See *straight* in Index of the *English Dialect Grammar.* (Wright's notation changed to IPA. Wright gives the pronunciation as follows: [straχt, strāχt, stræiχt, streχt, strōχt].) Wright's instance of *strait* as a Scottish form of *straight* refers to the verb rather than the adjective, is limited to one particular place, and seems indeed to be based upon an error, or at least a confusion of the two words. He gives *strait* as a form of *straight,* with reference to Jamieson (see *EDD*). Jamieson, however, does not consider this the origin of the word, and, though his derivations are not always acceptable, he is in this case probably correct. His entry reads: "To STRAIT,

gives *straucht* 'straight, direct,' *stret* 'strait, narrow; steep; in want of.' Scotland has retained the [χ]-sound of the original form of *straight*, and there is in consequence little possibility of confusion between this word and *strait*, which never had that sound. And in this area, where the two have been consistently differentiated, both are living words in present-day dialects.

In England the differentiation is not always maintained. But several considerations are of particular significance, in any survey of the appearance in dialect of the two words.

To begin with, *strait* 'narrow' is a living term in districts that are for the most part Northern and North Midland, that is, where the [χ]-sound in *straight* was pronounced for a longer time than in Southern areas. It was, indeed, preserved in the [streiχt] forms until into the 19th century (see above), and this in itself is enough to account for the persistence in those areas of the word *strait*. In the South and East Midlands, the very districts where we should expect early French loan-words to persist, the two became homonyms through the early disappearance in those areas of [χ], and one, the French borrowing, has passed out of ordinary use.

And existing data, though incomplete and therefore unsatisfactory, bear out this general conclusion. It cannot be denied that the two do exist as homonyms in certain districts. Haigh's *Dialect of the Huddersfield District* gives [streit] 'straight, not bent' and [streit], [stre:t] 'strait, narrow, strict.'[22] Distinction between the two is not striking, at times does not exist. Wright's records in the *English Dialect Dictionary* and the *English Dialect Grammar*, also, indicate the same thing, [e:] and [e] being given as the vowel-sound in *straight* within the area in which *strait* [stre:t, stret] appears:[23] in east Warwick, in northeast Yorkshire, southeast Yorkshire (but see below), in northwest and southeast Lancashire, in north Leicestershire, and central Northamptonshire (see Map 5, p. 109). But differentiation is more common than strict homonymy, as the same records show. In a large part of the area where the vowel-sound in *strait* is recorded as a monophthong, [e:] or [e], that in *straight* is a diphthong, [ei]. And in six or seven specific districts of England differentiation as distinct as that in Scotland can be pointed out. In part of central Lancashire and in southeast Yorkshire *straight* 'not bent' appears in the form [sθreit]. This is a normal dialectal development in east Yorkshire (and perhaps in Lancashire)[24] shared, apparently, by *straight* but not, for some

v.a. To straighten, to tighten, Aberd. O.Fr. *stret*, *streit*, *stroit*, reserré, étroit; Lat. *stringere*, *strict-us*."

22. Haigh's notation changed. He gives [streit], with [ei] as in *reign*; [strēt], with [ē] as in *mate*.

23. Wright's notation changed.

24. See the numerous instances listed by Wright in the *EDD* of words in str- and tr- which appear in e.Yks. (and occasionally in Lancashire) in sthr- forms: *sthreea*

reason, by *strait*. It separates the two words distinctly. In central and north-central Yorkshire *straight* is pronounced [striət]. In east Yorkshire, in one section, it is [stri:t]. In north and south Durham, and in several districts contiguous to the area where *strait* 'narrow' is a living word, for example in northwest Lincolnshire and north Herefordshire, *straight* is pronounced [strait]. Each of these is distinct from the [stre:t, stret] pronunciations that Wright gives as common for *strait*.[25] To these may be added the differentiation noted between the words by the collector of dialect terms of Leicestershire. He gives: "Straightaway (pron. streetawee), adv. var. of 'straightway' immediately"; "Streetawee, adv., var. pron. of 'straightway'"; and

Stret, adj., var. pron. of "strait," narrow; tight; close; "hard up"; short of. "As we're so stret for speakers to-dee," was the commencement of an oration at an agricultural dinner. "Ah stooffed 'im [a bull-finch] so stret as it med all 'is feathers stan' oop."[26]

Though it is not yet consistently carried out, there is to be noted a marked impulse in the dialects where both words are preserved to use them in forms which are not easily confused.

In the South and the East Midlands, homonymy developed early, as the result of the loss of the [χ]-sound in *straight*. In these sections, *strait* has disappeared as a word in general use. Dialects do not offer proof of this homonymy as readily as does the standard language, for records are less detailed. *Strait* has disappeared, and comparison of its phonetic value with that of *straight* in these areas is impossible. But it is significant that in several widely distributed sections outside the part of the country where *strait* 'narrow' persists, the vowel-sound in *straight*, in dialect,[27] coincides with that in *faith* and in *pray*, in both of which words the *ai* is to be traced to the same Old French sound that is represented in *strait* 'narrow.'[28] (See Map 6, p. 111, and the table in Note 28 below.)

In Scotland, where normal language developments differentiated *straight* and *strait*, the two exist together to the present day. In the North and the North Midlands of England the two were for long and are even now usually distinguished in sound, and both exist today. In the South and in the East Midlands of England, and in Standard

(straw), *sthreean* (strain), *sthritch* (stretch), *sthramash* (stramash), *sthrade* (strode), *sthriddle* (striddle), *sthraddle* (straddle), *thravel* (travel), *sthring* (string), etc.

25. Wright's phonetic notation is changed in this section to IPA.

26. A. B. Evans and S. Evans (collector and editor), *Leicestershire Words, Phrases, and Proverbs,* English Dialect Society, Series C, Original Glossaries, London, 1881. See the Glossary and p. 10: ". . . *ee* as in 'meet.'" *Stret* [stret].

27. Records for pronunciation of this word are unusually full.

28. The coincidence of the sounds in these words is not universal. Variant pronunciations of both exist at times; at times they differ entirely. But the following brief table, constructed from Wright's records (but in IPA symbols), indicates that

English, where homonymy developed early, one of the words has gone out of use. The general situation supports the conclusion that homonymy and ensuing confusion were detrimental to *strait* 'narrow.'

the number of places where the sounds are identical is not negligible, is even considerable. (See also Map 6.)

District	Straight	Faith	Pray
Kent	[strait]	se. [faiθ]	se. [prai]
Wilts.	w. [strait]	me. [faiθ]	me. w. [prai]
Dorset	e. [strait]	[faiθ]	[prai]
W. Somerset	[strait]	[faiθ]	
S. Nhb.	[streit]	[feiθ]	
N. Staffords.	[strɛət]	[fɛəθ]	[prɛə]
Lincolns.	m. s. [strɛət]	[fɛəθ]	[prɛə]
S. Oxfords.	[strɛət]	[fɛəθ]	
Sussex	e. [strɛət]	[fɛəθ]	
N. Cumb.	[striət]	[fiəθ]	
S. Worc.	[strait]		[prai]
Rutlands.	[stre:t]		[pre:]

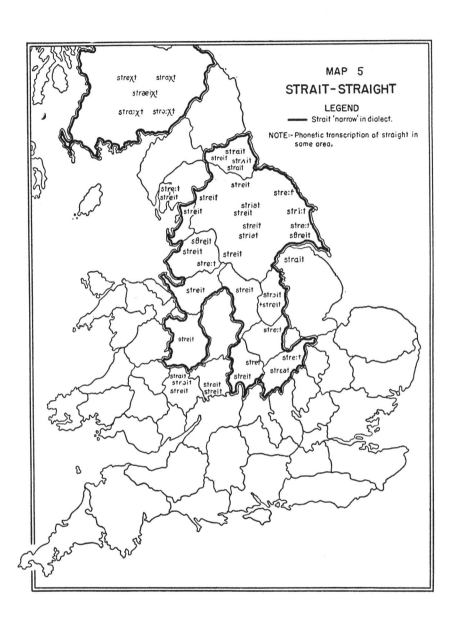

MAP 5

STRAIT-STRAIGHT

LEGEND

—— Strait 'narrow' in dialect.

NOTE:- Phonetic transcription of straight in some area.

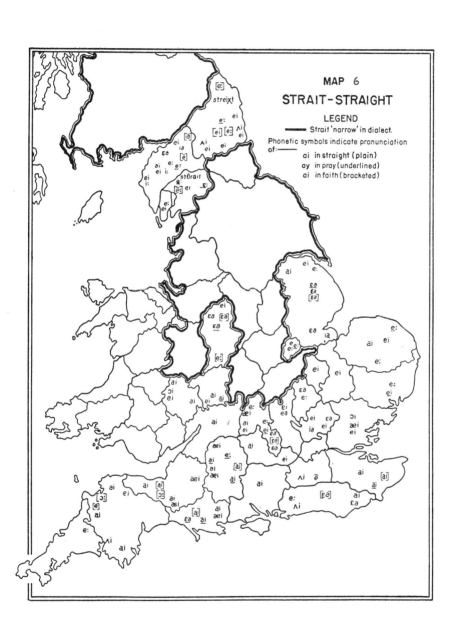

MAP 6

STRAIT-STRAIGHT

LEGEND

—— Strait 'narrow' in dialect.

Phonetic symbols indicate pronunciation
of:——

ai in straight (plain)
ay in pray (underlined)
ai in faith (bracketed)

VI

Conflict of Churn *and* Chirm

CONFLICT between words is brought about in various ways, not always by normal phonetic change or by foreign importations that clash with native words. An interesting case is that between *churn* and *chirm*, which involves dialects alone, not occurring in Standard English, where the two remain consistently different in form and pronunciation, so far as both appear.

In a portion of the Midlands and the Southwest of England, through the devious ways of dialect, the word *churn*, sb. and v., 'a machine for making butter,' 'to make butter,' and *chirm* 'the noise of birds or voices,' as verb 'to cry out, to chatter noisily, to talk glibly, to fret, complain' became homonyms in the forms *churm, chirm* [tʃəː(r)m] and were thus subject to confusion the one with the other in communities where both were used. "There was a churm outside the door": one making such a remark and meaning 'a confused, intermingled noise or hum' might have to explain that he did not mean 'a churn.' "Ben had been churmin aal the daay."[1] Since [tʃəː(r)m] means both 'to churn' and 'to murmur, fret, find fault, complain,' the statement is ambiguous. Confusion was to be expected if both were used in the same communities. But confusion has been avoided in this case. The present geographical distribution of the various forms of the two words offers a striking demonstration of the ways in which language avoids such situations.

Churn 'a machine for making butter,' 'to make butter' is a common English word. As a substantive it existed in Old English as *cyrn*, *cyrin*, for *cirn, *ciern, a common Germanic word. The corresponding verb is not recorded in Old English but first appears in the records of the *NED* in the 15th century. The initial *c* of OE *cyrn* was palatal [tʃ] (Jordan's *tš*. Cf. Jordan, § 179), as is proved by the later development of the word. OE *y* in accented syllables usually appears in Modern English derivatives as *i*, instead of the *e* peculiar to Kent and the Southeast, or the *u* which developed from *y* in the West Midlands but which was replaced by the unrounded *i* after the 14th century.[2] But in *cyrn* the neighboring consonants favored rounding,[3] and the word entered Standard English as *churn* (with *u* from *ü* from OE *y, ie*), with variants *chirne, cherne, chyrne* appearing from the

---

1. Wright, *EDD* under *Churm* 'to churn,' in Somerset.
2. Luick, *Hist. Gram.*, § 287.
3. Luick, *Hist. Gram.*, § 397; also Wright, *EMEGr.*, § 126.

15th century through the 17th. The vowel-sound in Modern English in each case is the same.[4]

The same vowel-sound [ə:] was kept in the two main dialectal forms that the word assumed. From the 14th century, it has existed in the North of England and in Scotland in the form *kirn*, variants *kern, kurn, kyrn*.[5] In the Midlands and South *churn* appears in the interesting form *churm*, already mentioned. Such forms in final *-m* (*churm(e, chearme*) are recorded as early as the 16th century in the *NED* and are common today in an area embracing some nine counties: Nottinghamshire, Leicestershire, Northamptonshire, southeast Worcestershire, Herefordshire, Gloucestershire, Oxfordshire, Somerset, Wiltshire[6] (see Map 7, p. 117).

Churn is a word familiar to English-speaking people everywhere. *Chirm*, sb. and v., on the other hand, is an archaic word in Standard English and a dialectal word, though it was originally used widely. It means 'noise, din, chatter, the mingled din or noise of many birds or voices' and 'to cry out, to chatter noisily, to talk glibly, to fret, complain,' with other connected senses listed in Wright's *EDD*. It is connected with OE *cirman* 'to cry out, shout, make a noise,' and derived from OE *cirm, cyrm, cierm* 'a cry, shout, uproar.' OE *cierm, cirm* gave ME *chirm*, with the same vowel-sound as that in *churn*.[7] The *ie* before *r* in *cierm* appeared as later *i, e,* or *u*,[8] hence modern *chirm, cherm, churm*. In all three of these spellings the word appears in dialects of the present day—*cherm* in Berkshire and Devon, *churm* in Scotland, Northumberland, and Hampshire, *chirm* more widely. (See Wright, *EDD*, and the map for this study.) And a fourth variant spelling is of unusual interest. *Charm* 'the blended singing or noise of many birds; the song or singing of birds or of men' is a dialectal form appearing from 1548 on (see *NED, Charm* sb.[2]), and found now in a group of southern and western counties in England. (See the map for this study.) The *NED* says:

[*Charm* is a] dialectal variant of *cherme*, a common 16th c. form of *chirm*. . . . Perhaps some fancied association with *Charm* sb.[1], or with L. *carmen*, may have contributed to give this form its literary standing;

4. Henry Cecil Wyld, *A Short History of English* (3d ed., New York, 1927), § 252: "ME *ŭ before r or r* + *consonant: becomes* [a], *which becomes* [ʌ] . . . ; as the [r] sound weakened the vowel was lengthened, and ultimately made into a flat vowel, fully lengthened, giving present-day [ʌ]." ME *er* (so far as it did not become *ar*) and ME *ir* developed into the same [ʌ]-sound (see § 228 and § 256). Wyld's [a] is IPA [ʌ], his [ʌ] is IPA [ə:].

5. Sometimes in the history of these sounds in Scottish certain grades were retained which passed, in Standard English, into the later [ə:]. Wyld, *Short History of English*, § 256.

6. See Wright, *EDD*.

7. See Wyld, *Short History of English*, § 252, § 256. ME *i* + *r* or *r* + consonant became ME [ʌ], Mod E [ə:] and *u* + *r* or *r* + consonant became ME [ʌ], MnE [ə:].

8. Luick, *Hist. Gram.*, § 287.

for an original *chirm* would naturally give later *cherm* and *churm,* but not *charm.* . . .

There was, however, an OE word *cearm* 'clamor, noise,' which is surely the source of MnE *charm* 'noise of singing.'[9]

It is the use made of the word in dialects that throws further light on the ways in which languages and dialects avoid confusion between homophones. At this point the map will most easily present the circumstances. In nine counties of the Midlands and the Southwest (Somerset, Wiltshire, Gloucester, Hereford, Worcester, Oxford, Northampton, Leicester, Nottingham) *churm* is the dialectal form of *churn* 'to make butter, etc.' Contiguous to this area on three sides —in Devon to the southwest, in Berkshire and Hampshire to the south, and in East Anglia to the east—and in one small section within the counties just named, that is, south Worcestershire, appear areas in which the homonym *chirm* 'noise of voices, to chatter, to fret, etc.' is in general dialectal use. (See map.) Only in south Worcestershire do the two overlap, though it might be supposed from the relative position of the four *chirm* 'noise' areas that the word was once used throughout much of this Midland and southern section. And the fact that the word is known, though in a variant form, in all the area where the meaning 'churn' is expressed in the form *churm* except the two northernmost counties, Nottinghamshire and Leicestershire, strengthens the possibility of this assumption. But in all the area (except the two counties just mentioned) where *churm* [tʃəːrm] or [tʃəːm] means 'churn' and in several counties all closely bordering upon this section, *chirm* [tʃəː(r)m] meaning 'noise,' 'to chatter,' appears in the form *charm* [tʃɑːrm]. The homonyms did not remain unchanged in the same areas. *Ben has been churmin aal tha daay* means 'Ben has been churning.' *The children are charmin on the doorstep* in the same community means 'they are chattering noisily.' The speakers of dialect of these sections of England avoided the inconvenience of possible confusion between two words alike in sound, with meanings capable of conflict, by choosing, consciously or unconsciously, a variant form for one of them which is distinct phonetically from the other. By means of the form *charm* confusion between *churm* 'to churn' and *chirm* 'to chatter, to complain' has been made impossible.

There is another extensive section in the North, comprising Scotland and the three counties of Northumberland, Cumberland, Durham, in which *chirm,* sb. and v., is a living dialectal word. There was

9. This statement is based on a note written by Professor Max Förster, of Munich, on the present study. His full comment follows: "*NED* overlooks that there is already an OE form *čearm* 'noise,' without umlaut, which may be the basis of *cherm* and *charm.* B.T. *Suppl.* Also, Cymric *garm* points to a P.Gmc. *garmōn (OE *cearm*) besides *garmi (OE *cyrm, cierm,* for older OE *čearmi-.*"

here no possibility of confusion with forms of *churn*, for *churn* in Scotland and the North of England exists in forms with initial *k-* —*kirn, kern*, etc. The *k-* is due probably to Scandinavian influence; *kirna* in Old Norse has the same meanings as English *churn*.

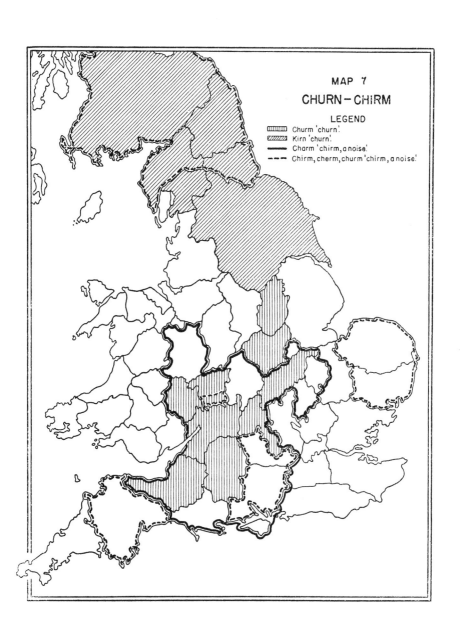

MAP 7
CHURN - CHIRM

LEGEND
Churm 'churn'.
Kirn 'churn'.
Charm 'chirm, a noise'.
Chirm, cherm, churm 'chirm, a noise'.

BIBLIOGRAPHY

Works on Linguistic Geography

BRANYS, E., *Homonyme Substantive im Neuenglischen*, Berlin, 1938.

BRIDGES, ROBERT, *On English Homophones*, Society for Pure English, Tract II, Oxford, 1919.

BULACHOVSKIJ, L. A., "De l'Homonymie dans les langues slaves," *Revue des Études Slaves*, VIII (1928), 68–80.

DAUZAT, ALBERT, *Essais de géographie linguistique, Noms d'animaux*, Paris, 1921.

DAUZAT, ALBERT, *Essais de géographie linguistique*, Deuxième Série, Paris, 1928.

DAUZAT, ALBERT, *Essais de géographie linguistique*, Nouvelle Série, Montpelier and Paris, 1938.

DAUZAT, ALBERT, *La géographie linguistique*, Paris, 1922.

FRINGS, THEODOR, "Sprachgeographie und Kulturgeographie," *Zeitschrift für Deutschkunde*, XLIV (1930), 546–62.

FRINGS, THEODOR, *Studien zur Dialektgeographie des Niederrheins zwischen Düsseldorf und Aachen*, Deutsche Dialektgeographie, V, Marburg, 1913.

GAMILLSCHEG, ERNST, *Die Sprachgeographie und ihre Ergebnisse für die allgemeine Sprachwissenschaft*, Neuphilologische Handbibliothek für die westeuropäischen Kulturen und Sprachen, II, Bielefeld and Leipzig, 1928.

GAMILLSCHEG, ERNST, "Wetzstein und Kumpf im Galloromanischen," *Archivum Romanicum*, VI (1922), 1–104.

GILLIÉRON, JULES, *L'Aire* CLAVELLUS, *d'après l'Atlas linguistique de la France*, Neuveville, 1912.

GILLIÉRON, JULES, *Généalogie des mots qui désignent l'Abeille, d'après l'Atlas linguistique de la France*, Paris, 1918.

GILLIÉRON, JULES and J. MONGIN, *Étude de géographie linguistique*, SCIER *dans la Gaule Romane du Sud et de l'Est*, Paris, 1905.

GILLIÉRON, JULES and MARIO ROQUES, *Études de géographie linguistique d'après l'Atlas linguistique de la France*, Paris, 1912.

HEMKEN, EMIL, *Das Aussterben alter Substantiva im Verlaufe der englischen Sprachgeschichte*, Kiel, 1906.

HOLTHAUSEN, F., "Vom Aussterben der Wörter," *Germanisch-Romanische Monatsschrift*, VII (1915–19), 184–96.

HUBER, JOSEPH, "Sprachgeographie, Ein Rückblick und Ausblick," *Bulletin de Dialectologie Romane*, I (1909), 89–117.

IORDAN, I. and J. ORR, *An Introduction to Romance Linguistics*, London, 1937.

JABERG, KARL, *Aspects géographiques du langage*, Société de Publications Romanes et Françaises, XVIII, Paris, 1936.

JABERG, KARL, "Die neuere Forschung auf dem Gebiete der romanischen

Sprachgeographie," *Die Geisteswissenschaften*, xviii (1914), 488–93.

JABERG, KARL, *Sprachgeographie. Beitrag zum Verständnis des Atlas linguistique de la France*, Aarau, 1908.

JABERG, KARL, "Sprachgeographische Untersuchungen," *Archiv für das Studium der neueren Sprachen und Literaturen*, cxx (1908), 96–8.

JABERG, KARL, "Wie der Hundedachs zum Dachs und der Dachs zum Iltis Wird," in *Festschrift für Ernst Tappolet*, Basel, 1935.

JACOBSEN, LIS, "Om Ordenes Død," *Arkiv för Nordisk Filologi*, xxxi (1914–15), 236–84.

JAESCHKE, KURT, *Beiträge zur Frage des Wortschwundes im Englischen*, Breslau, 1931.

JUD, J., "Probleme der altromanischen Wortgeographie," *Zeitschrift für Romanische Philologie*, xxxviii (1917), 1–75.

JUD, J., "Problèmes de géographie linguistique romane," *Revue de Linguistique Romane*, i (1925), 181–236.

KRETSCHMER, PAUL, *Wortgeographie der hochdeutschen Umgangssprache*, Göttingen, 1918.

KUEN, H., "Beobachtungen an einem kranken Wort," in *Festschrift für Ernst Tappolet*, Basel, 1935.

LIEBICH, B., "Kleine Beiträge zur deutschen Wortforschung," in H. Paul and W. Braune's *Beiträge zur Geschichte der Deutschen Sprache und Literatur*, xxiii (1898), 223–31.

MEILLET, A., *J. Gilliéron et l'influence de l'étude des parlers locaux sur le développement du Romanisme*, Paris, 1926.

MENNER, ROBERT J., "The Conflict of Homonyms in English," *Language*, xii (1936), 229–44.

NOREEN, ADOLF, "Ordens död," *Spridda Studier*, Andra Samlingen, Stockholm, 1903.

OBERDÖRFFER, WILHELM, *Das Aussterben altenglischer Adjektive und ihr Ersatz im Verlaufe der englischen Sprachgeschichte*, Kiel, 1908.

ÖHMANN, E., "Die Präposition AFTER im Deutschen," in *PBB*, lv (1931), 230–43.

ÖHMANN, E., *Über Homonymie und Homonyme im Deutschen*, in *Annales Academiæ Scientiarum Fennicæ*, Ser. B. 32.1 (Helsinki, 1934), 1–143.

OFFE, JOHANNES, *Das Aussterben alter Verba und ihr Ersatz im Verlaufe der englischen Sprachgeschichte*, Kiel, 1908.

PESSLER, WILHELM, "Deutsche Wortgeographie," *Wörter und Sachen*, xv (1933), 1–80.

RICHTER, ELISE, "Über Homonymie," in *Festschrift für . . . Paul Kretschmer*, Vienna, etc., 1926.

ROEDDER, EDWIN, "Linguistic Geography," *Germanic Review*, i (1926), 281–308.

SCHRIJNEN, JOSEF, *Essai de bibliographie de géographie linguistique générale*, Nimègue, 1933.

TEICHERT, FRIEDRICH, *Über das Aussterben alter Wörter im Verlaufe der englischen Sprachgeschichte*, Erlangen, 1912.

TERRACHER, L. A., *Étude de géographie linguistique. Les Aires morpho-

logiques dans les parlers populaires du nord-ouest de l'Angoumois (*1800–1900*), Paris, 1914.

TERRACHER, L. A., *L'Histoire des langues et la géographie linguistique,* Oxford, 1929.

TRNKA, B., "Bemerkungen zur Homonymie," *Travaux du Cercle Linguistique de Prague,* IV (1931), 152–6.

WREDE, FERDINAND (ed.), *Deutsche Dialektgeographie,* Marburg, 1908 sqq.

Dictionaries and Glossaries

ATKINSON, J. C., *A Glossary of the Cleveland Dialect,* London, 1868.

BOSWORTH, JOSEPH, *An Anglo-Saxon Dictionary,* edited by T. N. Toller, Oxford, 1882–98.

BOSWORTH, JOSEPH, *An Anglo-Saxon Dictionary. Supplement* by T. N. Toller, Oxford, 1921.

CRAIGIE, SIR WILLIAM and J. R. HULBERT (eds.), *Dictionary of American English on Historical Principles,* Chicago, 1938 sqq.

DARTNELL, GEORGE E. and E. H. GODDARD, *A Glossary of Words Used in the County of Wiltshire,* English Dialect Society, Series C, Original Glossaries, No. 69, London, 1893.

DICKINSON, W. and E. W. PREVOST, *A Glossary of the Words and Phrases Pertaining to the Dialect of Cumberland,* London and Carlisle, 1899.

EVANS, SEBASTIAN (ed.), *Leicestershire Words, Phrases, and Proverbs,* collected by A. B. Evans, English Dialect Society, Series C, Original Glossaries, London, 1881.

FALK, H. S. and ALF TORP, *Norwegisch-Dänisches etymologisches Wörterbuch,* Heidelberg, 1910–11.

GILLIÉRON, JULES, *Atlas linguistique de la France,* NOTICE *servant à l'intelligence des cartes,* Paris, 1902.

GILLIÉRON, JULES and E. EDMONT, *Atlas linguistique de la France,* Paris, 1902–10. (Referred to as *ALF.*)

GRANT, WILLIAM (ed.), *The Scottish National Dictionary,* Edinburgh, 1931 sqq.

HAIGH, W. E., *A New Glossary of the Dialect of the Huddersfield District,* London, 1928.

HALL, JOHN R. CLARK, *A Concise Anglo-Saxon Dictionary,* 3d ed., Cambridge, 1931.

HOLTHAUSEN, F., *Altenglisches etymologisches Wörterbuch,* Heidelberg, 1934.

JAMIESON, JOHN, *An Etymological Dictionary of the Scottish Language,* rev. by J. Longmuir and D. Donaldson, Paisley, 1879 sqq.

MARSHALL, W. H., *Provincialisms of East Yorkshire,* English Dialect Society, Series B, Reprinted Glossaries ed. by W. W. Skeat, Part I, No. 2, London, 1873.

MORRIS, M. C. F., *Yorkshire Folk-Talk,* London and York, 1892.

MURRAY, J. A. H. *et al.* (eds.), *New English Dictionary on Historical Principles,* Oxford, 1888 sqq. Also edition of 1933. (Referred to as *NED.*)

PEASE, SIR ALFRED E., *A Dictionary of the Dialect of the North Riding of Yorkshire,* Whitby, 1928.

RAY, JOHN, *A Collection of English Words Not Generally Used, with Their Significations and Original: In Two Alphabetical Catalogues: The One of Such as are Proper to the Northern, the Other to the Southern Counties,* English Dialect Society, Series B, Reprinted Glossaries ed. by W. W. Skeat, Part III, Nos. 15 and 16, London, 1874.

ROBINSON, F. K., *A Glossary of Words Used in the Neighbourhood of Whitby,* English Dialect Society, Series C, Original Glossaries, London, 1875 and 1876.

RYE, WALTER, *A Glossary of Words Used in East Anglia, Founded on That of Forby,* English Dialect Society, Series C, No. 75, London, 1895.

SKEAT, W. W., *Nine Specimens of English Dialects,* English Dialect Society, No. 76, London, 1896.

STRATMANN, F. H., *A Middle-English Dictionary,* Oxford, 1891.

WILLAN, ROBERT, *A List of Ancient Words at Present Used in the Mountainous District of the West Riding of Yorkshire,* English Dialect Society, Series B, Reprinted Glossaries ed. by W. W. Skeat, Part I, No. 7, London, 1873.

WREDE, FERDINAND (ed.), *Deutscher Sprachatlas, auf Grund des von Georg Wenker begründeten Sprachatlas des Deutschen Reichs,* Marburg, 1926 sqq.

WRIGHT, JOSEPH (ed.), *The English Dialect Dictionary,* London, etc., 1898 sqq. (Referred to as *EDD.*)

WYLD, HENRY CECIL (ed.), *The Universal Dictionary of the English Language,* London, 1932.

General Works

BACH, ADOLF, *Deutsche Mundartforschung, Ihre Wege, Ergebnisse und Aufgaben,* Heidelberg, 1934.

BJÖRKMAN, ERIK, *Scandinavian Loan-Words in Middle English,* Part I, Halle, 1900; Part II, Halle, 1902.

BLOOMFIELD, LEONARD, *Language,* New York, 1933.

BRADLEY, HENRY, *The Collected Papers of Henry Bradley,* Oxford, 1928.

DARMESTETER, ARSÈNE, *La Vie des mots, Étudiée dans leurs significations,* Paris, 1895.

DAUZAT, ALBERT, *La Vie du langage,* Paris, 1922.

DIKE, EDWIN B., "Obsolete English Words, Some Recent Views," *Journal of English and Germanic Philology,* XXXIV (1935), 351–65.

DIKE, EDWIN B., "Obsolete Words," *Philological Quarterly,* XII (1933), 207–19.

DIKE, EDWIN B., "Our Oldest Obsoletisms," *Englische Studien,* LXVIII (1933–34), 339–50.

ELLIS, ALEXANDER, *On Early English Pronunciation, with Especial Reference to Shakspere and Chaucer,* EETS, Extra Series II, Part 5, London, 1889.

English Dialect Society Publications.

FEIST, ROBERT, *Studien zur Rezeption des französischen Wortschatzes im Mittelenglischen, Beiträge zur englischen Philologie*, xxv, Leipzig, 1934.

GAUCHAT, L., "Interferenzen," in *Festschrift für Ernst Tappolet*, Basel, 1935.

GILLIÉRON, JULES, *Étude sur la défectivité des verbes. La Faillite de l'étymologie phonétique*, Neuveville, 1919.

GILLIÉRON, JULES, *Les Étymologies des étymologistes et celles du peuple*, Paris, 1922.

GILLIÉRON, JULES, *Pathologie et thérapeutique verbales*, Paris, 1921.

GRANT, WILLIAM, *The Pronunciation of English in Scotland*, Cambridge, 1913.

GRANT, WILLIAM and JAMES M. DIXON, *Manual of Modern Scots*, Cambridge, 1921.

JESPERSEN, OTTO, *A Modern English Grammar on Historical Principles*, 3d and 5th eds., Heidelberg and London, 1927, 1931, 1933.

JESPERSEN, OTTO, "Monosyllabism in English," in *Linguistica*, Copenhagen, 1933.

JORDAN, RICHARD, *Handbuch der mittelenglischen Grammatik*, Heidelberg, 1925.

KÖKERITZ, HELGE, *The Phonology of the Suffolk Dialect*, Uppsala, 1932.

LUICK, KARL, *Historische Grammatik der englischen Sprache*, Leipzig, 1921 sqq.

LUICK, KARL, *Studien zur englischen Lautgeschichte*, Vienna and Leipzig, 1903.

LUICK, KARL, *Untersuchungen zur englischen Lautgeschichte*, Strassburg, 1896.

METTIG, ROBERT, *Die französischen Elemente im Alt- und Mittelenglischen (800–1258)*, Marburg, 1910.

NAUMANN, H., "Über das sprachliche Verhältnis von Ober- zu Unterschicht," *Jahrbuch für Philologie (Idealistische Philologie)*, 1 (1925), 55–69.

ORTON, HAROLD, *The Phonology of a South Durham Dialect*, London, 1933.

SAPIR, EDWARD, "Sound Patterns in Language," *Language*, 1 (1925), 37–51.

WRIGHT, JOSEPH, *The English Dialect Grammar*, Oxford, etc., 1905. (*EDGr.*)

WRIGHT, JOSEPH, *A Grammar of the Dialect of Windhill, in the West Riding of Yorkshire*, English Dialect Society, Series C, No. 67, London, 1892.

WRIGHT, JOSEPH and ELIZABETH M. WRIGHT, *An Elementary Middle English Grammar*, London, etc., 1923. (*EMEGr.*)

WYLD, HENRY CECIL, *A Short History of English*, 3d ed., New York, 1927.

ZIPF, G. K., *The Psycho-Biology of Language*, Boston, 1935.

INDEX